Elizabeth Parsons Ware Packard

Marital Power Exemplified in Mrs. Packard's Trial

And Self-Defence from the Charge of Insanity - Three Years' Imprisonment for Religious Belief, by the Arbitrary Will of a Husband

MARITAL POWER EXEMPLIFIED

IN

Mrs. Packard's Trial,

AND

SELF-DEFENCE FROM THE CHARGE OF INSANITY;

OR

Three Years' Imprisonment for Religious Belief,

BY THE

ARBITRARY WILL OF A HUSBAND,

WITH

AN APPEAL TO THE GOVERNMENT TO SO CHANGE THE LAWS

AS TO AFFORD

Legal Protection to Married Women.

BY MRS. E. P. W. PACKARD.

CHICAGO:
CLARKE & CO., PUBLISHERS.
1870.

TABLE OF CONTENTS.

	Page
Introduction,	3
The Great Trial of Mrs. Elizabeth P. W. Packard, who was confined Three Years in the State Asylum of Illinois, charged by her Husband, Rev. Theophilus Packard, with being Insane. Her discharge from the Asylum, and subsequent Imprisonment at her own House by her Husband. Her release on a Writ of Habeas Corpus, and the question of her Sanity tried by a Jury. Her Sanity fully established,	13
Narrative of events continued,	42
Miscellaneous questions answered,	61
False Reports corrected,	85
Note of thanks to my Patrons and the Press,	107
Testimonials,	117
Conclusion,	126
An Appeal to the Government,	130

Entered, according to Act of Congress, in the year 1866, by
MRS. E. P. W. PACKARD,
In the Clerk's Office of the District Court of the District of Connecticut.

INTRODUCTION.

A BRIEF narrative of the events which occasioned the following Trial seems necessary as an Introduction to it, and are here presented for the kind reader's candid consideration. It was in a Bible-class in Manteno, Kankakee County, Illinois, that I defended some religious opinions which conflicted with the Creed of the Presbyterian Church in that place, which brought upon me the charge of insanity. It was at the invitation of Deacon Dole, the teacher of that Bible-class, that I consented to become his pupil, and it was at his special request that I brought forward my views to the consideration of the class. The class numbered six when I entered it, and forty-six when I left it. I was about four months a member of it. I had not the least suspicion of danger or harm arising in any way, either to myself or others, from thus complying with his wishes, and thus uttering some of my honestly cherished opinions. I regarded the principle of religious tolerance as the vital principle on which our government was based, and I in my ignorance supposed this right was protected to all American citizens, even to the wives of clergymen. But, alas! my own sad experience has taught me the danger of believing a lie on so vital a question. The result was, I was legally kidnapped and imprisoned three years simply for uttering these opinions under these circumstances.

I was kidnapped in the following manner.—Early on the morning of the 18th of June, 1860, as I arose from my bed, preparing to take my morning bath, I saw my husband approaching my door with our two physicians, both members of his church and of our Bible-class,— and a stranger gentleman, sheriff Burgess. Fearing exposure I hastily locked my door, and proceeded with the greatest dispatch to dress myself. But before I had hardly commenced, my husband forced an entrance into my room through the window with an axe! And I, for shelter and protection against an exposure in a state of almost entire nudity, sprang into bed, just in time to receive my unexpected guests. The trio approached my bed, and each doctor felt my pulse, and without asking a single question both pronounced me insane. So it seems that in the estimation of these two M. D's, Dr. Merrick and Newkirk, insanity is indicated by the action of the pulse instead of the mind! Of course, my pulse was bounding at the time from excessive fright; and I ask, what lady of refinement and fine and tender sensibilities would not have a quickened pulse by such an untimely, unexpected, unmanly, and even outrageous entrance into her private sleeping room? I say it would be impossible for any woman, unless she was either insane or insensible to her surroundings, not to be agitated under such circumstances. This was the only medical examination I had. This was the only trial of *any kind* that I was allowed to have, to prove the charge of insanity brought against me by my husband. I had no chance of *self defence* whatever. My husband then informed me that the "forms of law" were all complied with, and he therefore requested me to dress myself for a ride to Jacksonville, to enter the Insane Asylum as an inmate. I objected, and protested against being imprisoned *without any trial*. But to no purpose. My husband insisted upon it that I had no protection in the law, but himself, and that he was doing by me just as the laws of the State allowed him to do. I could not then credit this statement, but now *know* it to be too sadly true; for the Statute of Illinois expressly states that a man may put his wife into an Insane Asylum without evidence of insanity. This law now stands on the 26th page, section 10, of the Illinois statute book, under the general head of "charities"! The law was passed February 15, 1851.

I told my husband I should not go voluntarily into the Asylum, and leave my six children and my precious babe of eighteen months, without some kind of trial; and that the law of force, brute force, would be the only power that should thus put me there. I then begged of him to handle me gently, if he was determined to force me, as I was easily hurt, and should make no physical resistance. I was soon in the hands of the sheriff, who forced me from my home by ordering two men to carry me to the wagon which took me to the depot. Esquire Labrie, our nearest neighbor, who witnessed this scene, said he was willing to testify before any court under oath, that " Mrs. Packard was literally kidnapped." I was carried to the cars from the depot in the arms of two strong men, whom my husband appointed for this purpose, amid the silent and almost speechless gaze of a large crowd of citizens who had collected for the purpose of rescuing me from the hands of my persecutors. But they were prevented from executing their purpose by the lie Deacon Dole was requested by my husband to tell the excited crowd, viz: that "The Sheriff has legal papers to defend this proceeding," and they well knew that for them to resist the Sheriff, the laws would expose themselves to imprisonment. The Sheriff confessed afterwards to persons who are now willing to testify under oath, that he told them that he did not have a sign of a legal paper with him, simply because the probate court refused to give him any, because, as they affirmed, he had not given them one evidence of insanity in the case. Sheriff Burgess died while I was incarcerated.

When once in the Asylum I was beyond the reach of all human aid, except what could come through my husband, since the law allows no one to take them out, except the one who put them in, or by his consent; and my husband determined never to take me out, until I recanted my new opinions, claiming that I was incurably insane so long as I could not return to my old standpoint of religious belief. Of course, I could not believe at my option, but only as light and evidence was presented to my own mind, and I was too conscientious to act the hypocrite, by professing to believe what I could not believe. I was therefore pronounced "hopelessly insane," and in about six weeks from the date of my imprisonment, my husband made his arrangements to have me, henceforth, legally regarded as hopelessly insane. In this defenceless, deplorable condition I lay closely imprisoned three years, being never allowed to step my foot on the ground after the first four months. At the expiration of three years, my oldest son, Theophilus, became of age, when he immediately availed himself of his manhood, by a legal compromise with his father and the trustees, wherein he volunteered to hold himself wholly responsible for my support for life, if his father would only consent to take me out of my prison. This proposition was accepted by Mr. Packard, with this proviso: that if ever I returned to my own home and children he should put me in again for life. The Trustees had previously notified Mr. Packard that I must be removed, as they should keep me no longer. Had not this been the case, my son's proposition would doubtless have been rejected by him.

The reasons why the Trustees took this position was, because they became satisfied that I was not a fit subject for that institution, in the following manner: On one of their official visits to the institution, I coaxed Dr. McFarland, superintendent of the Asylum, to let me go before them and "fire a few guns at Calvinism," as I expressed myself, that they might know and judge for themselves whether I deserved a life-long imprisonment for indulging such opinions. Dr. Mc Farland replied to my request, that the Trustees were Calvinists, and the chairman a member of the Presbyterian Synod of the United States.

"Never mind," said I, "I dont care if they are, I am not afraid to defend my opinions even before the Synod itself. I dont want to be locked up here all my lifetime without doing something. But if they are Calvinists," I added, "you may be sure they will call me insane, and then you will have them to back you up in your opinion and position respecting me." This argument secured his consent to let me go before them. He also let me have two sheets of paper to write my opinions upon. With my document prepared, "or gun loaded," as I called it, and examined by the Doctor to see that all was right, that is, that it contained no exposures of himself, I entered the Trustees' room, arm in arm with the Doctor, dressed in as attractive and tasteful a style as my own wardrobe and that of my attendant's would permit. Mr. Packard was present, and he said to my friends afterwards that he never saw his wife look so "sweet and attractive" as I then did. After being politely and formally introduced to the Trustees, individually, I was seated by the chairman, to receive his permission to speak, in the following words: "Mrs. Packard, we have heard Mr. Packard's statement, and the Doctor said you would like to speak for yourself. We will allow you ten minutes for that purpose."

I then took out my gold watch, (which was my constant companion in my prison,) and looking at it, said to the Doctor, "please tell me if I overgo my limits, will you?" And then commenced reading my document in a quiet, calm, clear, tone of voice. It commenced with these words: "Gentlemen, I am accused of teaching my children doctrines ruinous in their tendency, and such as alienate them from their father. I reply, that my teachings and practice both, are ruinous to Satan's cause, and do alienate my children from Satanic influences. I teach Christianity, my husband teaches Calvinism. They are antagonistic systems and uphold antagonistic authorities. Christianity upholds God's authority; Calvinism the devil's authority," &c., &c.

Thus I went on, most dauntlessly and fearlessly contrasting the two systems, as I viewed them, until my entire document was read, without being interrupted, although my time had more than expired.

Confident I had secured their interest as well as attention, I ventured to ask if I might be allowed to read another document I held in my hand, which the Doctor had not seen. The request was voted upon and met not only with an unanimous response in the affirmative, but several cried out: "Let her go on! Let us hear the whole!" This document bore heavily upon Mr. Packard and the Doctor both. Still I was tolerated. The room was so still I could have heard a clock tick. When I had finished, instead of then dismissing me, they commenced questioning me, and I only rejoiced to answer their questions, being careful however not to let slip any chance I found to expose the darkest parts of this foul conspiracy, wherein Mr. Packard and their Superintendent were the chief actors. Packard and McFarland both sat silent and speechless, while I fearlessly exposed their wicked plot against my personal liberty and my rights. They did not deny or contradict one statement I made, although so very hard upon them both.

Thus nearly one hour was passed, when Mr. Packard was requested to leave the room. The Doctor left also, leaving me alone with the Trustees. These intelligent men at once endorsed my statements, and became my friends. They offered me my liberty at once, and said that anything I wanted they stood ready to do for me. Mr. Brown, the Chairman, said he saw it was of no use for me to go to my husband; but said they would send me to my children if I wished to go, or to my father in Massachusetts, or they would board me up in Jacksonville. I thanked them for their kind and generous offers; "but," said I, "it is of no use for me to accept of any one of them, for I am still Mr. Packard's wife, and there is no law in America to protect a wife from her husband. I am not safe from him outside these walls, on this continent, unless I flee to Canada; and there, I don't know as a fugitive wife is safe from her husband. The truth is, he is determined to keep me in an Asylum prison as long as I live, if it can be done; and since no law prevents his doing so, I see no way for me but to live and die in this prison. I may as well die here as in any other prison."

These manly gentlemen apprehended my sad condition and expressed their real sympathy for me, but did not know what to advise me to do. Therefore they left it to me and the Doctor to do as we might think best. I suggested to the Doctor that I write a book, and in this manner lay my case before the People—the government of the United States—and ask for the protection of the laws. The Doctor fell in with this suggestion, and I accordingly wrote my great book of seven hundred pages, entitled "The Great Drama,—An Allegory," the first installment of which is already in print and six thousand copies in circulation. This occupied me nine months, which completed my three years of prison life.

The Trustees now ordered Mr. Packard to take me away, as no one else could legally remove me. I protested against being put into his hands without some protection, knowing, as I did, that he intended to incarcerate me for life in Northampton Asylum, if he ever removed me from this. But, like as I entered the Asylum against my will, and in spite of my protest, so I was put out of it into the absolute power of my persecutor again, against my will, and in spite of my protest to the contrary.

I was accordingly removed to Granville, Putnam County, Illinois, and placed in the family of Mr. David Field, who married my adopted sister, where my son paid my board for about four months. During this time, Granville community became acquainted with me and the facts in the case, and after holding a meeting of the citizens on the subject the result was, that Sheriff Leaper was appointed to communicate to me their decision; which was, that I go home to my children taking their voluntary pledge as my protection; that, should Mr. Packard again attempt to imprison me without a trial, that they would use their influence to get him imprisoned in a penitentiary, where they thought the laws of this Commonwealth would place him. They presented me thirty dollars also to defray the expenses of my journey home to Manteno. I returned to my husband and little ones, only to be again treated as a lunatic. He cut me off from communication with this community, and my other friends, by intercepting my mail; made me a close prisoner in my own house; refused me interviews with friends who called to see me, so that he might meet with no interference in carrying out the plan he had devised to get me incarcerated again for life. This plan was providentially disclosed to me, by some letters he accidentally left in my room one night, wherein I saw that I was to be entered, in a few days, into Northampton Insane Asylum for life; as one of these letters from Doctor Prince, Superintendent of that Asylum, assured me of this fact. Another from his sister, Mrs. Marian Severance, of Massachusetts, revealed the mode in which she advised her brother to transfer me from my home prison to my Asylum prison. She advised him to let me go to New York, under the pretence of getting my book published, and have him follow in a train behind, assuring the conductors that I must be treated as an insane person, although I should deny the charge, as all insane persons did, and thus make sure of their aid as accomplices in this conspiracy against my personal liberty. The conductor must be directed to switch me off to Northampton, Mass., instead of taking me to New York, and as my through ticket would indicate to me that all was right, she thought this could be done without arousing my suspicions; then engage a carriage to transport me to the Asylum under the pretext of a hotel, and then lock me up for life as a state's pauper! Then, said she, you will have her out of the way, and can do as you please with her property, her children, and even her wardrobe; don't, says she, be even responsible this time for her clothing. (Mr. Packard was responsible for my body clothing in Jacksonville prison, but for nothing else. I was supported there three years as a state pauper. This fact, Mr. Packard most adroitly concealed from my rich father and family relatives, so that he could persuade my deluded father to place more of my patrimony in his hands, under the false pretense that he needed it to make his daughter more comfortable in the Asylum. My father sent him money for this purpose, supposing Mr. Packard was paying my board at the Asylum.)

Another letter was from Dr. McFarland, wherein I saw that Mr. Packard had made application for my readmission there, and Dr. McFarland had consented to receive me again as an insane patient! But the Trustees put their veto upon it, and would not consent to his plea that I be admitted there again. Here is his own statement, which I copied from his own letter: "Jacksonville, December 18, 1863. Rev. Mr. Packard, Dear Sir: The Secretary of the Trustees has probably before this communicated to you the result of their action in the case of Mrs. Packard. It is proper enough to state that I favored her readmission"! Then follows his injunction to Mr. Packard to be sure not to publish any thing respecting the matter. Why is this? Does an upright course seek or desire concealment? Nay, verily: It is conscious guilt alone that seeks concealment, and dreads agitation lest his crimes be exposed. Mine is only one of a large class of cases, where he has consented to readmit a sane person, particularly the wives of men, whose influence he was desirous of securing for the support of himself in his present lucrative position.

Yes, many intelligent wives and mothers did I leave in that awful prison, whose only hope of liberty lies in the death of their lawful husbands, or in a change of the laws, or in a thorough ventilation of that institution. Such a ventilation is needed, in order that justice be done to that class of miserable inmates who are now unjustly confined there.

When I had read these letters over three or four times, to make it sure I had not mistaken their import, and even took copies of some of them, I determined upon the following expedient as my last and only resort, as a self defensive act.

There was a stranger man who passed my window daily to get water from our pump. One day as he passed I beckoned to him to take a note which I had pushed down through where the windows come together, (my windows were firmly nailed down and screwed together, so that I could not open them,) directed to Mrs. A. C. Haslett, the most efficient friend I knew of in Manteno, wherein I informed her of my imminent danger, and begged of her if it was possible in any way to rescue me to do so, forthwith, for in a few days I should be beyond the reach of all human help. She communicated these facts to the citizens, when mob law was suggested as the only available means of rescue which lay in their power to use, as no law existed which defended a wife from a husband's power, and no man dared to take the responsibility of protecting me against my husband. And one hint was communicated to me clandestinely that if I would only break through my window, a company was formed who would defend me when once outside our house. This rather unlady like mode of self defence I did not like to resort to, knowing as I did, if I should not finally succeed in this attempt, my persecutors would gain advantage over me, in that I had once injured property, as a reason why I should be locked up. As yet, none of my persecutors had not the shadow of capital to make out the charge of insanity upon, outside of my opinions; for my conduct and deportment had uniformly been kind, lady-like and Christian; and even to this date, January, 1866, I challenge any individual to prove me guilty of one unreasonable or insane act. The lady-like Mrs. Haslett sympathized with me in these views; therefore she sought council of Judge Starr of Kankakee City, to know if any law could reach my case so as to give me the justice of a trial of any kind, before another incarceration. The Judge told her that if I was a prisoner in my own house, and any were willing to take oath upon it, a writ of habeas corpus might reach my case and thus secure me a trial. Witnesses were easily found who could take oath to this fact, as many had called at our house to see that my windows were screwed together on the outside, and our front outside door firmly fastened on the outside, and our back outside door most vigilantly guarded by day and locked by night. In a few days this writ was accordingly executed by the Sheriff of the county, and just two days before Mr. Packard was intending to start with me for Massachusetts to imprison me for life in Northampton Lunatic Asylum, he was required by this writ to bring me before the court and give his reasons to the court why he kept his wife a prisoner. The reason he gave for so doing was, that I was Insane. The Judge replied, "Prove it!" The Judge then empannelled a jury of twelve men, and the following Trial ensued as the result. This trial continued five days. Thus my being made a prisoner at my own home was the only hinge on which my personal liberty for life hung, independent of mob law, as there is no law in the State that will allow a married woman the right of a trial against the charge of insanity brought against her by her husband; and God only knows how many innocent wives and mothers my case represents, who have thus lost their liberty for life, by this arbitrary power, unchecked as it is by no law on the Statute book of Illinois.

THE GREAT TRIAL

OF

MRS. ELIZABETH P. W. PACKARD,

WHO WAS CONFINED FOR THREE YEARS IN THE STATE ASYLUM, OF ILLINOIS, CHARGED BY HER HUSBAND, REV. THEOPHILUS PACKARD, WITH BEING INSANE. HER DISCHARGE FROM THE ASYLUM, AND SUBSE-
QUENT IMPRISONMENT AT HER OWN HOUSE BY HER HUSBAND. HER RELEASE ON A WRIT OF
Habeas Corpus, AND THE QUESTION
OF HER SANITY TRIED
BY A JURY.
HER SANITY FULLY ESTABLISHED.

A FULL REPORT OF THE TRIAL, INCIDENTS, ETC.

BY STEPHEN R. MOORE, ATTORNEY AT LAW.

IN preparing a report of this trial, the writer has had but one object in view, namely, to present a faithful history of the case as narrated by the witnesses upon the stand, who gave their testimony under the solemnity of an oath. The exact language employed by the witnesses, has been used, and the written testimony given in full, with the exception of a letter, written by Dr. McFarland, to Rev. Theophilus Packard, which letter was retained by Mr. Packard, and the writer was unable to obtain a copy. The substance of the letter is found in the body of the report, and has been submitted to the examination of Mr. Packard's counsel, who agree that it is correctly stated.

This case was on trial before the Hon. Charles R. Starr, at Kankakee City, Illinois, from Monday, January 11th, 1864, to Tuesday the 19th, and came up on an application made by Mrs. Packard, under the *Habeas Corpus Act*, to be discharged from imprisonment by her husband in their own house.

The case has disclosed a state of facts most wonderful and startling. Reverend Theophilus Packard came to Manteno, in Kankakee county, Illinois, seven years since, and has remained in charge of the Presbyterian Church of that place until the past two years.

In the winter of 1859 and 1860, there were differences of opinion between Mr. Packard and Mrs. Packard, upon matters of religion, which resulted in prolonged and vigorous debate in the home circle. The heresies maintained by Mrs. Packard were carried by the husband from the fireside to the pulpit, and made a matter of inquiry by the church, and which soon resulted in open warfare; and her views and propositions were misrepresented and animadverted upon, from the pulpit, and herself made the subject of unjust criticism. In the Bible Class and in the Sabbath School, she maintained her religious tenets, and among her kindred and friends, defended herself from the obloquy of her husband.

To make the case fully understood, I will here remark, that Mr. Packard was educated in the Calvinistic faith, and for twenty-nine years has been a preacher of that creed, and would in no wise depart from the religion of his fathers. He is cold, selfish and illiberal in his views, possessed of but little talent, and a physiognomy innocent of expression. He has large self-will, and his stubbornness is only exceeded by his bigotry.

Mrs. Packard is a lady of fine mental endowments, and blest with a liberal education. She is an original, vigorous, masculine thinker, and were it not for her superior judgment, combined with native modesty, she would rank as a "strong-minded woman." As it is, her conduct comports strictly with the sphere usually occupied by woman. She dislikes parade or show of any kind. Her confidence that Right will prevail, leads her to too tamely submit to wrongs. She was educated in the same religious belief with her husband, and during the first twenty years of married life, his labors in the parish and in the pulpit were greatly relieved by the willing hand and able intellect of his wife.

Phrenologists would also say of her, that her self-will was large, and her married life tended in no wise to diminish this phrenological bump. They have been married twenty-five years, and have six children, the issue of their intermarriage, the youngest of whom was eighteen months old when she was kidnapped and transferred to Jacksonville. The older children have maintained a firm position against the abuse and persecutions of their father toward their mother, but were of too tender age to render her any material assistance.

Her views of religion are more in accordance with the liberal views of the age in which we live. She scouts the Calvinistic doctrine of man's total depravity, and that God has foreordained some to be saved and others to be damned. She stands fully on the platform of man's free agency and accountability to God for his actions. She believes that man, and nations, are progressive; and that in his own good time, and in accordance with His great purposes, Right will prevail over Wrong, and the oppressed will be freed from the oppressor. She believes slavery to be a national sin, and the church and the pulpit a proper place to combat this sin. These, in brief, are the points in her religious creed which were combatted by Mr. Packard, and were denominated by him as "emanations from the devil," or "the vagaries of a crazed brain."

For maintaining such ideas as above indicated, Mr. Packard denounced her from the pulpit, denied her the privilege of family prayer in the home circle, expelled her from the Bible Class, and refused to let her be heard in the Sabbath School. He excluded her from her friends, and made her a prisoner in her own house.

Her reasonings and her logic appeared to him as the ravings of a mad woman — her religion was the religion of the devil. To justify his conduct, he gave out that she was insane, and found a few willing believers, among his family connections.

This case was commenced by filing a petition in the words following, to wit:

STATE OF ILLINOIS, }ss.
KANKAKEE COUNTY.

To the Honorable CHARLES R. STARR, *Judge of the 20th Judicial Circuit in the State of Illinois.*

William Haslet, Daniel Beedy, Zalmon Hanford, and Joseph Younglove, of said county, on behalf of Elizabeth P. W. Packard, wife of Theophilus Packard, of said county, respectfully represent unto your Honor, that said Elizabeth P. W. Packard is unlawfully restrained of her liberty, at Manteno, in the county of Kankakee, by her husband, Rev. Theophilus Packard, being forcibly confined and imprisoned in a close room of the dwelling-house of her said husband, for a long time, to wit, for the space of four weeks, her said husband refusing to let her visit her neighbors and refusing her neighbors to visit her; that they believe her said husband is about to forcibly convey her from out the State; that they believe there is no just cause or ground for restraining said wife of her liberty; that they believe that said wife is a mild and amiable woman. And they are advised and believe, that said husband cruelly abuses and misuses said wife, by depriving her of her winter's clothing, this cold and inclement weather, and that there is no necessity for such cruelty on the part of said husband to said wife; and they are advised and believe, that said wife desires to come to Kankakee City, to make application to your Honor for a writ of *habeas corpus*, to liberate herself from said confinement or imprisonment, and that said husband refused and refuses to allow said wife to come to Kankakee City for said purpose; and that these petitioners make application for a writ of *habeas corpus* in her behalf, at her request. These petitioners therefore pray that a writ of *habeas corpus* may forthwith issue, commanding said Theophilus Packard to produce the body of said wife, before your Honor, according to law, and that said wife may be discharged from said imprisonment.

      (Signed) WILLIAM HASLET.
             DANIEL BEEDY.
J. W. ORR, } *Petitioners' Attorney.* ZALMON HANFORD.
H. LORING,   J. YOUNGLOVE.
   STEPHEN R. MOORE, *Counsel.*

STATE OF ILLINOIS, } ss.
KANKAKEE COUNTY.

 William Haslet, Daniel Beedy, Zalmon Hanford, and Joseph Younglove, whose names are subscribed to the above petition, being duly sworn, severally depose and say, that the matters and facts set forth in the above petition are true in substance and fact, to the best of their knowledge and belief.

           WILLIAM HASLET.
           DANIEL BEEDY
           ZALMON HANFORD.
           J. YOUNGLOVE.

Sworn to and subscribed before me, this }
11th day of January, A. D. 1864.
     MASON B. LOOMIS, *J. P.*

 Upon the above petition, the Honorable C. R. Starr, Judge as aforesaid, issued a writ of *habeas corpus*, as follows:

STATE OF ILLINOIS, } ss.
KANKAKEE COUNTY.

The People of the State of Illinois, To THEOPHILUS PACKARD

 WE COMMAND YOU, That the body of Elizabeth P. W. Packard, in your custody detained and imprisoned, as it is said, together with the day and cause of caption and detention, by whatsoever name the same may be called, you safely have before Charles R. Starr, Judge of the Twentieth Judicial Circuit, State of Illinois, at his chambers, at Kankakee City in the said county, on the 12th instant, at one o'clock,

P. M., and to do and receive all and singular those things which the said Judge shall then and there consider of her in this behalf, and have you then and there this writ.

Witness, Charles R. Starr, Judge aforesaid, this 11th day of January, A. D. 1864.

        CHARLES R. STARR, [SEAL.]
[Revenue Stamp.]   *Judge of the 20th Judicial Circuit of the State of Illinois.*

Indorsed: "By the *Habeas Corpus* Act."

To said writ, the Rev. Theophilus Packard made the following return:

The within named Theophilus Packard does hereby certify, to the within named, the Honorable Charles R. Starr, Judge of the 20th Judicial Circuit of the State of Illinois, that the within named Elizabeth P. W. Packard is now in my custody, before your Honor. That the said Elizabeth is the wife of the undersigned, and is and has been for more than three years past insane, and for about three years of that time was in the Insane Asylum of the State of Illinois, under treatment, as an insane person. That she was discharged from said Asylum, without being cured, and is incurably insane, on or about the 18th day of June, A. D. 1863, and that since the 23rd day of October, the undersigned has kept the said Elizabeth with him in Manteno, in this county, and while he has faithfully and anxiously watched, cared for, and guarded the said Elizabeth, yet he has not unlawfully restrained her of her liberty; and has not confined and imprisoned her in a close room, in the dwelling-house of the undersigned, or in any other place or way, but, on the contrary, the undersigned has allowed her all the liberty compatible with her welfare and safety. That the undersigned is about to remove his residence from Manteno, in this State, to the town of Deerfield, in the county of Franklin, in the State of Massachusetts, and designs and intends to take his said wife Elizabeth with him. That the undersigned has never misused or abused the said Elizabeth, by depriving her of her winter's clothing, but, on the contrary, the undersigned has always treated the said Elizabeth with kindness and affection, and has provided her with a sufficient quantity of winter clothing and other clothing; and that the said Elizabeth has never made any request of the undersigned, for liberty to come to Kankakee City, for the purpose of suing out a writ of *habeas corpus*. The undersigned hereby presents a letter from Andrew McFarland, Superintendent of the Illinois State Hospital, at Jacksonville, in this State, snowing her discharge, and reasons of discharge, from said institution, which is marked "A," and is made a part of this return. And also presents a certificate from the said Andrew McFarland, under the seal of said hospital, marked "C," refusing to re-admit the said Elizabeth again into said hospital, on the ground of her being incurably insane, which is also hereby made a part of this return.

THEOPHILUS PACKARD.
Dated *January* 12, 1864.

The Court, upon its own motion, ordered an issue to be formed, as to the sanity or insanity of Mrs. E. P. W. Packard, and ordered a venire of twelve men, to aid the court in the investigation of said issue. And thereupon a venire was issued.

The counsel for the respondent, Thomas P. Bonfield, Mason B. Loomis, and Hon. C. A. Lake, moved the court to quash the venire, on the ground that the court had no right to call a jury to determine the question, on an application to be discharged on a writ of *habeas corpus*. The court overruled the motion; and thereupon the following jury was selected:

John Stiles, Daniel G. Bean, V. H. Young, F. G. Hutchinson, Thomas Muncey, H. Hirshberg, Nelson Jarvais, William Hyer, Geo. H. Andrews, J. F. Mafet, Lemuel Milk, G. M. Lyons.

CHRISTOPHER W. KNOTT was the first witness sworn by the respondent, to maintain the issue on his part, that she was insane; who being sworn, deposed and said:

I am a practicing physician in Kankakee City. Have been in practice fifteen years. Have seen Mrs. Packard; saw her three or four years ago. Am not much acquainted with her. Had never seen her until I was called to see her at that time. I was called to visit her by Theophilus Packard. I thought her partially deranged on religious matters, and gave a certificate to that effect. I certified that she was insane upon the subject of religion. I have never seen her since.

Cross-examination.—This visit I made her was three or four years ago. I was there twice — one-half hour each time. I visited her on request of Mr. Packard, to determine if she was insane. I learned from him that he designed to convey her to the State Asylum. Do not know whether she was aware of my object, or not. Her mind appeared to be excited on the subject of religion; on all other subjects she was perfectly rational. It was probably caused by overtaxing the mental faculties. She was what might be called a monomaniac. Monomania is insanity on one subject. Three-fourths of the religious community are insane in the same manner, in my opinion. Her insanity was such that with a little rest she would readily have recovered from it. The female mind is more excitable than the male. I saw her perhaps one-half hour each time I visited her. I formed my judgment as to her insanity wholly from conversing with her. I could see nothing except an unusual zealousness and warmth upon religious topics. Nothing was said, in my conversation with her, about disagreeing with Mr. Packard on religious topics. Mr. Packard introduced the subject of religion the first time I was there: the second time, I introduced the subject. Mr. Packard and Mr. Comstock were present. The subject was pressed on her for the purpose of drawing her out. Mrs. Packard would manifest more zeal than most of people upon any subject that interested her. I take her to be a lady of fine mental abilities, possessing more ability than ordinarily found. She is possessed of a nervous temperament, easily excited, and has a strong will. I would say that she was insane, the same as I would say Henry Ward Beecher, Spurgeon, Horace Greely, and like persons, are insane. Probably three weeks intervened between the visits I made Mrs. Packard. This was in June, 1860.

Re-examined.—She is a woman of large, active brain, and nervous temperament. I take her to be a woman of good intellect. There is no subject which excites people so much as religion. Insanity produces, oftentimes, ill-feelings towards the best friends, and particularly the family, or those more nearly related to the insane person—but not so with monomania. She told me, in the conversation, that the Calvinistic doctrines were wrong, and that she had been compelled to withdraw from the church. She said that Mr. Packard was more insane than she was, and that people would find it out. I had no doubt that she was insane. I only considered her insane on that subject, and she was not bad at that. I could not judge whether it was hereditary. I thought if she was withdrawn from conversation and excitement, she could have got well in a short time. Confinement in any shape, or restraint, would have made her worse. I did not think it was a bad case; it only required rest.

J. W. BROWN, being sworn, said:

I am a physician; live in this city; have no extensive acquaintance with Mrs. Packard. Saw her three or four weeks ago. I examined her as to her sanity or insanity. I was requested to make a visit, and had an extended conference with her: I spent some three hours with her.

I had no difficulty in arriving at the conclusion, in my mind, that she was insane.

Cross-examination.—I visited her by request of Mr. Packard, at her house. The children were in and out of the room; no one else was present. I concealed my object in visiting her. She asked me if I was a physician, and I told her no; that I was an agent, selling sewing machines, and had come there to sell her one.

The first subject we conversed about was sewing machines. She showed no signs of insanity on that subject.

The next subject discussed, was the social condition of the female sex. She exhibited no special marks of insanity on that subject, although she had many ideas quite at variance with mine, on the subject.

The subject of politics was introduced. She spoke of the condition of the North and the South. She illustrated her difficulties with Mr. Packard, by the difficulties between the North and the South. She said the South was wrong, and was waging war for two wicked purposes: first, to overthrow a good government, and second, to establish a despotism on the inhuman principle of human slavery. But that the North, having right on their side, would prevail. So Mr. Packard was opposing her, to overthrow free thought in woman; that the despotism of man may prevail over the wife; but that she had right and truth on her side, and that she would prevail.

During this conversation I did not fully conclude that she was insane.

I brought up the subject of religion. We discussed that subject for a long time, and then I had not the slightest difficulty in concluding that she was hopelessly insane.

Question. Dr., what particular idea did she advance on the subject of religion that led you to the conclusion that she was hopelessly insane?

Answer. She advanced many of them. I formed my opinion not so much on any one idea advanced, as upon her whole conversation. She then said that she was the "Personification of the Holy Ghost." I did not know what she meant by that.

Ques. Was not this the idea conveyed to you in that conversation:— That there are three attributes of the Deity—the Father, the Son, and the Holy Ghost? Now, did she not say, that the attributes of the Father were represented in mankind, in man; that the attributes of the Holy Ghost were represented in woman; and that the Son was the fruit of these two attributes of the Deity?

Ans. Well, I am not sure but that was the idea conveyed, though I did not fully get her idea at the time.

Ques. Was not that a new idea to you in theology?

Ans. It was.

Ques. Are you much of a theologian?

Ans. No.

Ques. Then because the idea was a novel one to you, you pronounced her insane.

Ans. Well, I pronounced her insane on that and other things that exhibited themselves in this conversation.

Ques. Did she not show more familiarity with the subject of religion and the questions of theology, than you had with these subjects?

Ans. I do not pretend much knowledge on these subjects.

Ques. What else did she say or do there, that showed marks of insanity?

Ans. She claimed to be better than her husband — that she was right — and that he was wrong — and that all she did was good, and all he did was bad; that she was farther advanced than other people, and more nearly perfection. She found fault particularly that Mr. Packard would not discuss their points of difference on religion in an open, manly way, instead of going around and denouncing her as crazy to her friends and to the church.

She had a great aversion to being called insane. Before I got through the conversation she exhibited a great dislike to me, and almost treated me in a contemptuous manner. She appeared quite lady-like. She had a great reverence for God, and a regard for religious and pious people.

Re-examined. — *Ques.* Dr., you may now state all the reasons you have for pronouncing her insane.

Ans. I have written down, in order, the reasons which I had, to found my opinion on, that she was insane. I will read them.

1. That she claimed to be in advance of the age thirty or forty years.
2. That she disliked to be called insane.
3. That she pronounced me a copperhead, and did not prove the fact.
4. An incoherency of thought. That she failed to illuminate me and fill me with light.
5. Her aversion to the doctrine of the total depravity of man.
6. Her claim to perfection or nearer perfection in action and conduct.
7. Her aversion to being called insane.
8. Her feelings towards her husband.
9. Her belief that to call her insane and abuse her, was blasphemy against the Holy Ghost.

10. Her explanation of this idea.
11. Incoherency of thought and ideas.
12. Her extreme aversion to the doctrine of the total depravity of mankind, and in the same conversation, saying her husband was a specimen of man's total depravity.
13. The general history of the case.
14. Her belief that some calamity would befall her, owing to my being there, and her refusal to shake hands with me when I went away.
15. Her viewing the subject of religion from the osteric standpoint of Christian exegetical analysis, and agglutinating the polsynthetical ectoblasts of homogeneous asceticism.

The witness left the stand amid roars of laughter; and it required some moments to restore order in the court-room.

JOSEPH H. WAY, sworn, and said:

I am a practicing physician in Kankakee City, Illinois. I made a medical examination of Mrs. Packard a few weeks since, at her house; was there perhaps two hours. On most subjects she was quite sane. On the subject of religion I thought she had some ideas that are not generally entertained. At that time I thought her to be somewhat deranged or excited on that subject; since that time I have thought perhaps I was not a proper judge, for I am not much posted on disputed points in theology, and I find that other people entertain similar ideas. They are not in accordance with my views, but that is no evidence that she is insane.

Cross-examined.—I made this visit at her house, or his house, perhaps, at Manteno. I conversed on various subjects. She was perfectly sane on every subject except religion, and I would not swear now that she was insane. She seemed to have been laboring under an undue excitement on that subject. She has a nervous temperament, and is easily excited. She said she liked her children, and that it was hard to be torn from them. That none but a mother could feel the anguish she had suffered; that while she was confined in the Asylum, the children had been educated by their father to call her insane. She said she would have them punished if they called their own mother insane, for it was not right.

ABIJAH DOLE, sworn, and says:

I know Mrs. Packard; have known her twenty-five or thirty years. I am her brother-in-law. Lived in Manteno seven years. Mrs.

Packard has lived there six years. I have been sent for several times by her and Mr. Packard, and found her in an excited state of mind. I was there frequently; we were very familiar. One morning early, I was sent for: she was in the west room; she was in her night clothes. She took me by the hand and led me to the bed. Libby was lying in bed, moaning and moving her head. Mrs. Packard now spoke and said, "How pure we are." "I am one of the children of heaven; Libby is one of the branches."—"The woman shall bruise the serpent's head." She called Mr. Packard a devil. She said, Brother Dole, these are serious matters. If Brother Haslet will help me, we will crush the body. She said, Christ had come into the world to save men, and that she had come to save woman. Her hair was disheveled. Her face looked wild. This was over three years ago.

I was there again one morning after this. She came to me. She pitied me for marrying my wife, who is a sister to Mr. Packard; said I might find an agreeable companion. She said if she had cultivated amativeness, she would have made a more agreeable companion. She took me to another room and talked about going away; this was in June before they took her to the State Hospital. She sent for me again; she was in the east room; she was very cordial. She wanted me to intercede for Theophilus, who was at Marshall, Michigan; she wanted him to stay there, and it was thought not advisable for him to stay. We wished him to come away, but did not tell her the reasons. He was with a Swedenborgian.

After this I was called there once in the night. She said she could not live with Mr. Packard, and she thought she had better go away. One time she was in the Bible class. The question came up in regard to Moses smiting the Egyptian;. she thought Moses had acted too hasty, but that all things worked for the glory of God. I requested her to keep quiet, and she agreed to do it.

I have had no conversation with Mrs. Packard since her return from the Hospital; she will not talk with me because she thinks I think she is insane. Her brother came to see her; he said he had not seen her for four or five years. I tried to have Mrs. Packard talk with him, and she would not have anything to do with him because he said she was a crazy woman. She generally was in the kitchen when I was there, overseeing her household affairs.

I was superintendent of the Sabbath School. One Sabbath, just at the close of the school, I was behind the desk, and almost like a vision she appeared before me, and requested to deliver or read an address to the school. I was much surprised; I felt so bad, I did not know what to do. (At this juncture the witness became very much affected, and choked up so that he could not proceed, and cried so loud that he could be heard in any part of the court-room. When he became calm, he went on and said), I was willing to gratify her all I could, for I knew she was crazy, but I did not want to take the responsibility myself, so I put it to a vote of the school, if she should be allowed to read it. She was allowed to read it. It occupied ten or fifteen minutes in reading.

I cannot state any of the particulars of that paper. It bore evidence of her insanity. She went on and condemned the church, all in all, and the individuals composing the church, because they did not agree with her. She looked very wild and very much excited. She seemed to be insane. She came to church one morning just as services commenced, and wished to have the church act upon her letter withdrawing from the church immediately. Mr. Packard was in the pulpit. She wanted to know if Brother Dole and Brother Merrick were in the church, and wanted them to have it acted upon. This was three years ago, just before she was taken away to the hospital.

Cross-examined.—I supposed when I first went into the room that her influence over the child had caused the child to become deranged. The child was nine years old. I believed that she had exerted some mesmeric or other influence over the child, that caused it to moan and toss its head. The child had been sick with brain fever; I learned that after I got there. I suppose the mother had considerable anxiety over the child; I suppose she had been watching over the child all night, and that would tend to excite her. The child got well. It was sick several days after this; it was lying on the bed moaning and tossing its head; the mother did not appear to be alarmed. Mr. Packard was not with her; she was all alone; she did not say that Mr. Packard did not show proper care for the sick child. I suppose she thought Libby would die.

Her ideas on religion did not agree with mine, nor with my view of the Bible.

I knew Mr. Packard thought her insane, and did not want her to discuss these questions in the Sabbath School. I knew he had opposed her more or less. This letter to the church was for the purpose of asking for a letter from the church.

Question. Was it an indication of insanity that she wanted to leave the Presbyterian Church?

Answer. I think it strange that she should ask for letters from the church. She would not leave the church unless she was insane.

I am a member of the church—I believe the church is right. I believe everything the church does is right. I believe everything in the Bible..

Ques. Do you believe literally that Jonah was swallowed by a whale, and remained in its belly three days, and was then cast up?

Ans. I do.

Ques. Do you believe literally that Elijah went direct up to Heaven in a chariot of fire—that the chariot had wheels, and seats, and was drawn by horses?

Ans. I do—for with God all things are possible.

Ques. Do you believe Mrs. Packard was insane, and is insane?

Ans. I do.

I never read any of Swedenborg's works. I do not deem it proper for persons to investigate new doctrines or systems of theology.

Re-examined.—I became a Presbyterian eight years ago. I was formerly a Congregationalist; Mr. Packard was a Congregationalist.

Re-cross-examination.— Ques. Was it dangerous for you to examine the doctrines or theology embraced in the Presbyterian Church, when you left the Congregational Church, and joined it?

Ans. I will not answer so foolish a question.

Witness discharged.

JOSEPHUS B. SMITH, sworn, says:

Am aged fifty years; have known Mrs. Packard seven years. I cannot tell the first appearance of any abnormal condition of her mind. I first saw it at the Sabbath School. She came in and wished to read a communication. I do not recollect everything of the communication. She did not read the letter, but presented it to Brother Dole. She said something about her small children, and left. She seemed to be excited. There was nothing very unusual in her appearance. Her voice was rather excited; it could be heard nearly over the house. I merely recall the circumstance, but recollect scarce anything else. It was an unusual thing for any person to come in and read an address. I do not recollect anything unusual in her manner.

(At this stage of the trial, an incident occurred that for a time stopped all proceedings, and produced quite an excitement in the court-room; and this report would not be faithful if it were passed over unnoticed. Mrs. Dole, the sister of Mr. Packard, came in, leading the little daughter of Mrs. Packard, and in passing by the table occupied by Mrs. Packard and her counsel, the child stopped, went up to her mother, kissed and hugged her, and was clinging to her with all child-like fervor, when it was observed by Mrs. Dole, who snatched the child up—and bid it "come away from that woman;" adding, "She is not fit to take care of you—I have you in my charge;" and thereupon led her away. The court-room was crowded to its utmost, and not a mother's heart there but what was touched, and scarce a dry eye was seen. Quite a stir was made, but the sheriff soon restored order.)

Cross-examined.—I had charge of the Sunday School; am a member of Mr. Packard's church. I knew Mr. Packard had considered her insane; knew they had had difficulties. I was elected superintendent of the school in place of Brother Dole, for the special purpose of keeping Mrs. Packard straight.

SYBIL DOLE, sworn, and says—

I am Mr. Packard's sister; have known her twenty-five years. Her natural disposition is very kind and sweet. Her education is very good; her morals without a stain or blemish. I first observed a change in her after we came to Manteno. I had a conversation with her, when she talked an hour without interruption; she talked in a wild, excited manner; the subject was partly religion. She spoke of her own attainments; she said she had advanced in spiritual affairs. This was two or three years before she went to the Asylum.

The next time was when she was preparing to go to York State. She was weeping and sick. Her trunk was packed and ready to go, but Mr. Packard was sick. From her voice, and the manner she talked, I formed an opinion of her insanity. She talked on various points; the conversation distressed me very much; I could not sleep. She was going alone; we tried to persuade her not to go alone. She accused Mr. Packard very strangely of depriving her of her rights of conscience—that he would not allow her to think for herself on religious questions, because they disagreed on these topics. She made her visit to New York. The first time I met her after her return, her health was much improved; she appeared much better. In the course of a few weeks, she visited at my house.

At another time, one of the children came up, and wanted me to go down; I did so. She was very much excited about her son remaining at Marshall. She was wild. She thought it was very wrong and tyrannical for Mr. Packard not to permit her son to remain there. She said very many things which seemed unnatural. Her voice, manner and ways, all showed she was insane.

I was there when Mr. Baker came there, to see about Theophilus remaining at Marshall with him. She was calmer than she was the day before. She said that she should spend the day in fasting and prayer. She said he had came in unexpectedly, and they were not prepared to entertain strangers. She was out of bread, and had to make biscuit for dinner. (One gentleman in the crowd turned to his wife and said, "Wife, were you ever out of bread, and had to make biscuit for dinner? I must put you into an Insane Asylum! No mistake!") I occupied the same room and bed with her. She went to Mr. Packard's room, and when she returned, she said, that if her son was not permitted to remain at Marshall, it would result in a divorce. She got up several times during the night. She told me how much she enjoyed the family circle. She spoke very highly of Mr. Packard's kindness to her. She spoke particularly of the tenderness which had once existed between them. I did not notice anything very remarkable in her conduct toward Mr. Packard, until just before she was sent to the Hospital.

One morning afterward, I went to her house with a lady; we wanted to go in, and were admitted. She seemed much excited. She said, "You regard me insane. I will thank you to leave my room." This was two or three months before she was sent to Jacksonville. Mr. Packard went out. She put her hand on my shoulder, and said she would thank me to go out too. I went out.

I afterward wanted to take the baby home. One morning I went down to see her, and prepared breakfast for her. She appeared thankful, and complimented me on my kindness. She consented for me to take the child; I did so. In a short time, about ten days after, the other children came up, and said, that she wanted to take her own child. I took the child down. Her appearance was very wild. She was filled with spite toward Mr. Packard. She defied me to take the child again, and said that she would evoke the strong arm of the law to help her keep it.

At another time, at the table, she was talking about religion, when Mr. Packard remonstrated with her; she became angry, and told him she would talk what and when she had a mind to. She rose up from the table, and took her tea-cup, and left the room in great violence.

Cross-examined.—I am a member of Mr. Packard's church, and am his sister. He and I have often consulted together about Mrs. Packard. Mr Packard was the first to ever suggest that she was insane; after that, I would more carefully watch her actions to find out if she was insane. The religious doctrines she advanced were at variance with those entertained by our church. She was a good, neat, thrifty and careful housekeeper. She was economical; kept the children clean and neatly dressed. She was sane on all subjects except religion. I do not think she would have entertained these ideas, if she had not been insane. I do not think she would have wanted to have withdrawn from our church, and unite with another church, if she had not been insane. She said she would worship with the Methodists. They were the only other Protestant denomination that held service at Manteno at the time. I knew when she was taken to Jacksonville Hospital. She was taken away in the morning. She did not want to go; we thought it advisable for her to go.

SARAH RUMSEY, sworn, and says:

Have lived one week in Mrs. Packard's house. I was present at the interview when Mrs. Packard ordered us to leave the room. Mrs. Packard was very pale and angry. She was in an undress, and her hair was down over her face. It was 11 o'clock in the forenoon — I staid at the house; Mrs. Packard came out to the kitchen. She was dressed then. She said she had come to reveal to me what Mr. Packard was. She talked very rapidly; she would not talk calm. She said Mr. Packard was an arch deceiver; that he and the members of his church had made a conspiracy to put her into the Insane Asylum; she wanted me to leave the conspirators. Soon after dinner she said, "Come with me, I have something to tell you." She said she had a new revelation; it would soon be here; and that she had been chosen by God for a particular mission. She said that all who decided with her, and remained true to her, would be rewarded by the millennium, and if I would side with her, that I would be a chief apostle in the millennium. She wanted to go to Batavia, but that Mr. Packard would give her no money to take her there; that Mr. Packard called her insane. She started to go out, and Mr. Packard made her return; took her into Mr. Comstock's, and Mr. Comstock made her go home.

I saw her again when Libby had the brain fever. She was disturbed because the family called her insane. She and Libby were crying together; they cried together a long time. This was Tuesday. She would not let me into the room. The next morning while at breakfast Mr. Labrie passed the window and came in. He said that Georgie had been over for him, and said that they were killing his mother. She acted very strangely all the time; was wild and excited.

Cross-examined. — Knew Mr. Packard two years before I went 'here to live. He was the pastor of our church. I am a member of the church. I did not attend the Bible class. Brother Dole came to me and said somebody of the church should go there, and stay at the house, and assist in packing her clothes and getting her ready to take off to the Hospital, and stay and take care of the children. I consented to go; I heard that Brother Packard requested Brother Dole to come for me. I never worked out before. They had a French servant, before I went there; Mr. Packard turned her off when I came, the same day. I did not want to take Mrs. Packard away. I did not think she exhibited any very unusual excitement, when the men came here to take her away. Doctors Merrick and Newkirk were the physicians who came there with Sheriff Burgess. She did not manifest as much excitement, when being taken away, as I would have done, under the same circumstances; any person would have naturally been opposed to being carried away.

The church had opposed her, in disseminating her ideas in the church; I was opposed to her promulgating her religious ideas in the church; I thought them wrong, and injurious. I was present at the Sabbath School when she read the paper to the school; I thought that bore evidence of insanity. It was a refutation of what Mrs. Dixon had written; I cannot give the contents of the paper now.

I was present when she read a confession of her conduct to the church; she had had her views changed partially, from a sermon preached upon the subject of the sovereignty and immutability of God. I did not think it strange conduct that she changed her views; and never said so. This was in the spring before the June when they took her away.

The article she read in the school was by the permission of the school.

I was present when she presented a protest against the church for refusing to let her be heard; I have only an indistinct recollection of it; it was a protest because they refused to listen to her.

Mr. Dole was the only person who came to the house when she was taken away, except the men with Burgess.

She said that Mr. Packard had deprived her of the liberty of conscience in charging her to be insane, when she only entertained ideas new to him.

I thought it was an evidence of insanity, because she maintained these ideas. I do not know that many people entertain similar ideas I suppose a good many do not think the Calvinistic doctrine is right, they are not necessarily insane because they think so.

When she found I was going to stay in the house, and that the French servant had been discharged, she ordered me into the kitchen; before that, she had treated me kindly as a visitor.

I thought it was an evidence of insanity for her to order me into the kitchen; she ought to have known that I was not an ordinary servant. The proper place for the servant is in the kitchen at work, and not in the parlor; I took the place of the servant girl for a short time.

She wanted the flower beds in the front yard cleaned out, and tried to get Mr. Packard to do it; he would not do it. She went and put on an old dress and went to work, and cleaned the weeds out, and worked herself into a great heat. It was a warm day; she staid out until she was almost melted down with the heat.

Question. What did she do then?

Answer. She went to her room and took a bath, and dressed herself, and then lay down exhausted. She did not come down to dinner.

Ques. And did you think that was an evidence of insanity?

Ans. I did — the way it was done.

Ques. What would you have done under similar circumstances? Would you have set down in the clothes you had worked in?

Ans. No.

Ques. Probably you would have taken a bath and changed your clothes too. And so would any lady, would they not?

Ans. Yes.

Ques. Then would you call yourself insane?

Ans. No. But she was angry and excited, and showed ill-will. She was very tidy in her habits; liked to keep the house clean, and have her yard and flowers look well. She took considerable pains with these things.

I remained there until she was taken away; I approved taking her away; I deemed her dangerous to the church; her ideas were contrary to the church, and were wrong.

The baby was eighteen months old when she was taken away. She was very fond of her children and treated them very kindly. Never saw her misuse them. Never heard that she had misused them. Never heard that she was dangerous to herself or to her family. Never heard that she had threatened or offered to destroy anything, or injure any person.

JUDGE BARTLETT was next called to the stand.

Am acquainted with Mrs. Packard. Had a conversation with her on religious topics. We agreed very well in most things. She did not say she believed in the transmigration of souls; she said, some persons had expressed that idea to her, but she did not believe it. It was spoken of lightly. She did not say ever to me, that Mr. Packard's soul would go into an ox. She did not say anything about her being related to the Holy Ghost. I thought then, and said it, that religious subjects were her study, and that she would easily be excited on that subject. I could not see that she was insane. I would go no stronger than to say, that her mind dwelt on religious subjects. She could not be called insane, for thousands of people believe as she does, on religion.

MRS. SYBIL DOLE, recalled.

At the time she got up from the table she went out. She said, "I will have no fellowship with the unfruitful works of darkness. No! not so much as to eat with them."

Re-cross-examined. — Question. Did you deem that an evidence of insanity?

Answer. I did.

Ques. She called Mr. Packard the unfruitful works of darkness?

Ans. I suppose so.

Ques. Did she also include you?

Ans. She might have done so.

Ques. This was about the time that her husband was plotting to kidnap her, was it not?

Ans. It was just before she was removed to the Asylum.

Ques. He had been charging her with insanity, had he not, at the table?

Ans. He had.

The prosecution now wished to adjourn the court for ten days, to enable them to get Dr. McFarland, Superintendent of the State Hospital, who, they claimed, would testify that she was insane. Counsel stated, he had been telegraphed to come, and a reply was received, that he was in Zanesville, Ohio, and would return in about ten days. They claimed his testimony would be very important. This motion the counsel of Mrs. Packard opposed, as it was an unheard-of proceeding to continue a cause after the hearing was commenced, to enable a party to hunt up testimony.

The matter was discussed on each side for a considerable length of time, when the court held that the defense should go on with their testimony, and after that was heard, then the court would determine about continuing the case to get Dr. McFarland, and perhaps he could be got before the defense was through, and if so, he might be sworn; and held that the defense should go on now.

The counsel of Mrs. Packard withdrew for consultation, and in a brief time returned, and announced to the court that they would submit the case without introducing any testimony, and were willing to submit it without argument. The counsel for Mr. Packard objected to this, and renewed the motion for a continuance; which the court refused.

The counsel for Mr. Packard then offered to read to the jury a letter from Dr. McFarland, dated in the month of December, 1863, written to Rev. Theophilus Packard; and also a certificate, under the seal of the State Hospital at Jacksonville, certifying that Mrs. Packard was discharged from the institution in June, 1863, and was incurably insane, which certificate was signed by Dr. McFarland, the Superintendent. To the introduction of this to the jury, the counsel for Mrs. Packard objected, as being incompetent testimony, and debarred the defense of the benefit of a cross-examination. The court permitted the letter and certificate to be read to the jury.

These documents were retained by Rev. Theophilus Packard; and the reporter has been unable to obtain copies of them. The letter is dated in December, 1863, at the State Hospital, Jacksonville, Illinois, and written to Rev. Theophilus Packard, wherein Dr. McFarland writes him that Mrs. Packard is hopelessly insane, and that no possible good could result by having her returned to the Hospital; that the officers of the institution had done everything in their power to effect a cure, and were satisfied she could not be cured, and refused to receive her into the institution.

The certificate, under the seal of the Hospital, was a statement, dated in June, 1863, at Jacksonville, Illinois, setting forth the time (three years) that Mrs. Packard had been under treatment, and that she had been discharged, as beyond a possibility of being cured.

The above is the import of these documents, which the reporter regrets he cannot lay before the public in full.

The prosecution now announced that they closed their case.

DEFENSE.

J. L. SIMINGTON was the first witness called for the defense. Being sworn, he said.

I live in Manteno; lived there since 1859, early in the spring. Knew Rev. Mr. Packard and Mrs. Packard. First became acquainted with them in 1858; I was then engaged in the ministry of the Methodist Church. I have practiced medicine eleven years.

I was consulted as a family physician by Mrs. Packard in 1860. Was quite well acquainted with Mrs. Packard, and with the family. Lived fifty or sixty rods from their house. Saw her and the family almost daily. I did not see anything unusual in her, in regard to her mind. I never saw anything I thought insanity with her. So far as I know she was a sane woman. I have seen her since she came from the Hospital; have seen nothing since to indicate she was insane My opinion is, she is a sane woman.

No cross-examination was made.

Dr. J. D. MANN, sworn, and says:

I live in Manteno; have lived there nine years. Practiced medicine there six years. I am not very intimately acquainted with either Mr. or Mrs. Packard. Mr. Packard invited me to go to his house to have an interview with Mrs. Packard. I went at his request. He requested me to make a second examination, which I did. There had been a physician there before I went. The last time, he wanted me to meet Dr. Brown, of this city, there. This was late in November last. He introduced me to Mrs. Packard. I had known her before she was taken to the Hospital, and this was the first time I had seen her since she had returned. I was there from one to two hours. I then made up my mind, as I had made up my mind from the first interview, that I could find nothing that indicated insanity. I did not go when Dr. Brown was there. Mr. Packard had told me she was insane, and my prejudices were, that she was insane. He wanted a certificate of her insanity, to take East with him. I would not give it.

The witness was not cross-examined.

JOSEPH E. LABRIE, sworn, and says:

Have known Mrs. Packard six years; lived fifteen or twenty rods from their house. Knew her in spring of 1860. Saw her nearly every day — sometimes two or three times a day. I belong to the Catholic Church. Have seen her since her return from Jacksonville. I have seen nothing that could make me think her insane. I always said she was a sane woman, and say so yet.

Cross-examined.—I am not a physician. I am not an expert. She might be insane, but no common-sense man could find it out.

Re-examined.—I am a Justice of the Peace, and Notary Public. Mr. Packard requested me to go to his house and take an acknowledg ment of a deed from her. I went there, and she signed and acknowledged the deed. This was within the past two months.

Re-cross-examined.—I was sent for to go to the house in the spring of 1860. My wife was with me. It was about taking her to Jacksonville. Mrs. Packard would not come to the room where I was. I stayed there only about twenty minutes.

Have been there since she returned from the Hospital. The door to her room was locked on the outside. Mr. Packard said, he had made up his mind to let no one into her room.

The counsel for Mrs. Packard offered to read to the jury the following paper, which had been referred to by the witnesses, as evidence of Mrs. Packard's insanity, and which Deacon Smith refused to hear read. The counsel for Mr. Packard examined the paper, and admitted it was the same paper.

The counsel for Mrs. Packard then requested permission of the court for Mrs. Packard to read it to the jury, which was most strenuously opposed. The court permitted Mrs. Packard to read it to the jury. Mrs. Packard arose, and read in a distinct tone of voice, so that every word was heard all over the court-room.

HOW GODLINESS IS PROFITABLE

DEACON SMITH—A question was proposed to this class, the last Sabbath Brother Dole taught us, and it was requested that the class consider and report the result of their investigations at a future session. May I now bring it up? The question was this:

"Have we any reason to expect that a Christian farmer, *as a Christian*, will be any more successful in his farming operations, than an impenitent sinner—and if *not*, how is it that godliness is profitable unto all things? Or, in other words, does the *motive* with which one prosecutes his secular business, other things being equal, make any difference in the *pecuniary* results?"

Mrs. Dixon gave it as her opinion, at the time, that the motive *did* affect the pecuniary results.

Now the *practical* result to which this conclusion leads, is such as will justify us in our judging of Mrs. Dixon's true *moral* character, next fall, by her *success* in her farming operations this summer.

My opinion differs from hers on this point; and my *reasons* are here given in writing, since I deem it necessary for *me*, under the existing state of feeling toward me, to put into a written form *all* I have to say, in the class, to prevent misrepresentation.

Should I be appropriating an unreasonable share of time, as a pupil, Mr.

Smith, to occupy four minutes of your time in reading them? I should like very much to read them, that the class may pass their honest criticisms upon them.

AN ANSWER TO THE QUESTION.

I think we have no *intelligent* reason for believing that the motives with which we prosecute our secular business, have any influence in the *pecuniary* results.

My reasons are *common sense* reasons, rather than strictly Bible proofs, viz.: I regard man as existing in three distinct departments of being, viz., his physical or animal, his mental or intellectual, his moral or spiritual; and each of these three distinct departments are under the control of *laws*, peculiar to itself; and these different laws do not interchange with, or affect each other' department.

For instance, a very *immoral* man may be a very *healthy*, long-lived man; for, notwithstanding he violates the *moral* department, he may live in conformity to the *physical* laws of his animal nature, which secure to him his physical health. And, on the other hand, a very moral man may suffer greatly from a diseased body, and be cut off in the very midst of his usefulness by an early death, in consequence of having violated the physical laws of his animal constitution. But on the moral plane he is the *gainer*, and the immoral man is the *loser*.

So our success in business depends upon our conformity to *those laws* on which success depends—*not* upon the *motives* which act *only* on the moral plane.

On this ground, the Christian farmer has no more *reason* to expect success in his farming operations, than the impenitent sinner. In either case, the foundation for success must depend upon the degree of *fidelity* with which the *natural laws* are applied, which cause the natural result—*not* upon the *motives* of the operator; since these moral acts receive their penalty and reward on an entirely different plane of his being.

Now comes in the question, how then is it true, that "godliness is *profitable* unto all things," if godliness is no guarantee to success in business pursuits?

I reply, that the profits of godliness cannot mean, simply, *pecuniary* profits, because this would limit the gain of godliness to this world, alone; whereas, it is profitable not only for *this life*, but also for the *life to come*. Gain and loss, dollars and cents, are not the coins current in the spiritual world.

But happiness and misery are coins which are current in *both* worlds. Therefore, it appears to me, that happiness is the profit attendant upon godliness, and for this reason, a *practically godly* person, who lives in conformity to all the various laws of his entire being, may expect to secure to himself, as a natural result, a greater amount of happiness than the ungodly person.

So that, in this sense, "Godliness is profitable unto all things," to every department of our being.

MANTENO, March 22, 1860.   E. P. W. PACKARD.

Mrs. Packard then stated that the above was presented to the class, the 15th day of the following April, and was *rejected* by the teacher Deacon Smith, on the ground of its being irrelevant to the subject, since she had not confined herself to the Bible alone for proof of her position.

As she took her seat, a murmur of applause arose from every part of the room, which was promptly suppressed by the sheriff.

DANIEL BEEDY, sworn, and says:

I live in Manteno. Have known Mrs. Packard six years; knew her in the spring of 1860. I lived a mile and a half from them. Have seen her very frequently since her return from Jacksonville. Had many conversations with her before she was taken away, and since her return. She always appeared to me like a sane woman. I heard she was insane, and my wife and I went to satisfy ourselves. I went there soon after the difficulties in the Bible class.

She is not insane. We talked about religion, politics, and various matters, such as a grey-haired old farmer could talk about, and I saw nothing insane about her.

Mr. BLESSING, sworn, and says:

I live in Manteno; have known Mrs. Packard six years; knew her in the spring of 1860; lived eighty rods from their house. She visited at my house. I have seen her at church. She attended the Methodist church for a while after the difficulties commenced, and then I saw her every Sunday. I never thought her insane.

After the word was given out by her husband that she was insane, she claimed my particular protection, and wanted me to obtain a trial for her by the laws of the land, and such an investigation she said she was willing to stand by. She claimed Mr. Packard was insane, if any one was. She begged for a trial. I did not then do anything, because I did not like to interfere between man and wife. I never saw anything that indicated insanity. She was always rational Had conversations with her since her return. She first came to my house. She claimed a right to live with her family. She considered herself more capable of taking care of her family than any other person.

I saw her at Jacksonville. I took Dr. Shirley with me to test her insanity. Dr. Shirley told me she was not insane

Cross-examination waived.

Mrs. Blessing, sworn, and says:

Have known Mrs. Packard seven years; knew her in 1860. Lived near them; we visited each other as neighbors. She first came to our house when she returned from Jacksonville. I did not see anything that indicated that she was insane. I saw her at Jacksonville. She had the keys, and showed me around. I heard the conversation there with Dr. Shirley; they talked about religion; did not think she talked unnatural. When I first went in, she was at work on a dress for Dr. McFarland's wife. I saw her after she returned home last fall, quite often, until she was locked in her room. On Monday after she got home, I called on her; she was at work; she was cleaning up the feather beds; they needed cleaning badly. I went there afterward; her daughter let me in. On Saturday before the trial commenced, I was let into her room by Mr. Packard; she had no fire in it; we sat there in the cold. Mr. Packard had a handful of keys, and unlocked the door and let me in. Mrs. Hanford was with me. Before this, Mrs. Hanford and myself went there to see her; he would not let us see her; he shook his hand at me, and threatened to put me out.

Mrs. Haslet, sworn, and said:

Know Mrs. Packard very well; have known her since they lived in Manteno; knew her in the spring of 1860; and since she returned from Jacksonville, we have been on intimate terms. I never saw any signs of insanity with her. I called often before she was kidnapped and carried to Jacksonville, and since her return.

I recollect the time Miss Rumsey was there; I did not see anything that showed insanity. I called to see her in a few days after she returned from Jacksonville; she was in the yard, cleaning feather beds. I called again in a few days; she was still cleaning house. The house needed cleaning; and when I again called, it looked as if the mistress of the house was at home. She had no hired girl. I went again, and was not admitted. I conversed with her through the window; the window was fastened down. The son refused me admission. The window was fastened with nails on the inside, and by two screws, passing through the lower part of the upper sash and the upper part of the lower sash, from the outside. I did not see Mr. Packard this time.

Cross-examination.—She talked about getting released from her imprisonment. She asked if filing a bill of complaint would lead to a divorce. She said she did not want a divorce; she only wanted protection from Mr. Packard's cruelty. I advised her to not stand it quietly, but get a divorce.

Dr. Duncanson, sworn, and said:

I live here; am a physician; have been a clergyman; have been a practicing physician twenty-one years. Have known Mrs. Packard since this trial commenced. Have known her by general report for three years and upwards. I visited her at Mr. Orr's. I was requested to go there and have a conversation with her and determine if she was sane or insane. Talked three hours with her, on political, religious and scientific subjects, and on mental and moral philosophy. I was educated at and received diplomas from the University of Glasgow, and Anderson University of Glasgow. I went there to see her, and prove or disprove her insanity. I think not only that she is sane, but the most intelligent lady I have talked with in many years. We talked religion very thoroughly. I find her an expert in both departments, Old School and New School theology. There are thousands of persons who believe just as she does. Many of her ideas and doctrines are embraced in Swedenborgianism, and many are found only in the New School theology. The best and most learned men of both Europe and this country, are advocates of these doctrines, in one shape or the other; and some bigots and men with minds of small calibre may call these great minds insane; but that does not make them insane. An insane mind is a diseased mind. These minds are the perfection of intellectual powers, healthy, strong, vigorous, and just the reverse of diseased minds, or insane. Her explanation of woman representing the Holy Ghost, and man representing the male attributes of the Father, and that the Son is the fruit of the Father and the Holy Ghost, is a very ancient theological dogma, and entertained by many of our most eminent men. On every topic I introduced, she was perfectly familiar, and discussed them with an intelligence that at once showed she was possessed of a good education, and a strong and vigorous mind. I did not agree with her in sentiment on many things, but I do not call people insane because they differ from me, nor from a majority, even, of people. Many persons called Swedenborg insane. That is true; but he had the largest brain of any person during the age in which he lived; and no one now dares call him insane. You might with as much propriety call Christ insane, because he taught the people many new and strange things; or Galileo; or Newton; or Luther, or Robert Fulton; or Morse, who electrified the world; or Watts or a thousand others I might name. Morse's best friends for a long time thought him mad; yet there was a magnificent mind, the embodiment of health and vigor.

So with Mrs. Packard; there is wanting every indication of insanity that is laid down in the books. I pronounce her a sane woman, and wish we had a nation of such women.

This witness was cross-examined at some length, which elicited nothing new, when he retired

The defense now announced to the court that they had closed all the testimony they wished to introduce, and inasmuch as the case had occupied so much time, they would propose to submit it without argument. The prosecution would not consent to this arrangement.

The case was argued ably and at length, by Messrs. Loomis and Bonfield for the prosecution, and by Messrs. Orr and Loring on the part of the defense.

It would be impossible to give even a statement of the arguments made, and do the attorneys justice, in the space allotted to this report.

On the 18th day of January, 1864, at 10 o'clock, P. M., the jury retired for consultation, under the charge of the sheriff. After an absence of seven minutes, they returned into court, and gave the following verdict:

STATE OF ILLINOIS, } ss.
KANKAKEE COUNTY,

We, the undersigned, Jurors in the case of Mrs. Elizabeth P. W. Packard, alleged to be insane, having heard the evidence in the case, are satisfied that said Elizabeth P. W. Packard is SANE.

JOHN STILES, *Foreman.*	H. HIRSHBERG.
DANIEL G. BEAN.	NELSON JERVAIS.
F. G. HUTCHINSON.	WILLIAM HYER.
V. H. YOUNG.	GEO. H. ANDREWS
G. M. LYONS.	J. F. MAFIT.
THOMAS MUNCEY.	LEMUEL MILK.

Cheers rose from every part of the house; the ladies waved their handkerchiefs, and pressed around Mrs. Packard, and extended her their congratulations. It was sometime before the outburst of applause could be checked. When order was restored, the counsel for Mrs. Packard moved the court, that she be discharged. Thereupon the court ordered the clerk to enter the following order:

STATE OF ILLINOIS, } ss.
KANKAKEE COUNTY,

It is hereby ordered that Mrs. Elizabeth P. W. Packard be relieved from all restraint incompatible with her condition as a sane woman.

C. R. STARR,
Judge of the 20th Judicial Circuit of the State of Illinois
January 18, 1864.

Thus ended the trial of this remarkable case. During each day of the proceedings the court-room was crowded to excess by an anxious audience of ladies and gentlemen, who are seldom in our courts. The verdict of the jury was received with applause, and hosts of friends crowded upon Mrs. Packard to congratulate her upon her release.

During the past two months, Mr. Packard had locked her up in her own house, fastened the windows outside, and carried the key to the door, and made her a close prisoner. He was maturing a plan to immure her in an Asylum in Massachusetts, and for that purpose was ready to start on the Thursday before the writ was sued out, when his plan was disclosed to Mrs. Packard by a letter he accidentally dropped in her room, written by his sister in Massachusetts, telling him the route he should take, and that a carriage would be ready at the station to put her in and convey her to the Asylum.

Vigorous action became necessary, and she communicated this startling intelligence through her window to some ladies who had come to see her, and were refused admission into the house.

On Monday morning, and before the defense had rested their case, Mr. Packard left the State, bag and baggage, for parts unknown, having first mortgaged his property for all it is worth to his sister and other parties.

We cannot do better than close this report with the following editorial from the Kankakee Gazette, of January 21, 1864:

MRS. PACKARD.

The case of this lady, which has attracted so much attention and excited so much interest for ten days past, was decided on Monday evening last, and resulted, as almost every person thought it must, in a complete vindication of her sanity. The jury retired on Monday evening, after hearing the arguments of the counsel; and after a brief consultation, they brought in a verdict that Mrs. Packard is a *sane* woman.

Thus has resulted an investigation which Mrs. Packard has long and always desired should be had, but which her cruel husband has ever sternly refused her. She has always asked and earnestly pleaded for a jury trial of her case, but her relentless persecutor has ever turned a deaf ear to her entreaties, and flagrantly violated all the dictates of justice and humanity.

She has suffered the alienation of friends and relatives; the shock of a kidnapping by her husband and his posse when forcibly removed to the Asylum; has endured three years incarceration in that Asylum —upon the general treatment in which there is severe comment in the State, and which in her special case was aggravatingly unpleasant and ill-favored; returning to her home she found her husband's saintly blood still congealed, a winter of perpetual frown on his face, and the sad dull monotony of "insane, insane," escaping his lips in all his communications to and concerning her; her young family, the youngest of the four at home being less than four years of age, these children —over whose slumbers she had watched, and whose wailings she had hushed with all a mother's care and tenderness — had been taught to look upon her as insane, and they were not to respect the counsels or heed the voice of a maniac just loosed from the Asylum, doom scaled by official certificates.

Soon her aberration of mind led her to seek some of her better clothing carefully kept from her by her husband, which very woman-like act was seized by him as an excuse for confining her in her room, and depriving her of her apparel, and excluding her lady friends. Believing that he was about to again forcibly take her to an asylum, four responsible citizens of that village made affidavit of facts which caused the investigation as to her sanity or insanity. During the whole of the trial she was present, and counseled with her attorneys in the management of the case.

Notwithstanding the severe treatment she has received for nearly four years past, the outrages she has suffered, the wrong to her nature she has endured, she deported herself during the trial as one who is not only not insane, but as one possessing intellectual endowments of a high order, and an equipoise and control of mind far above the majority of human kind. Let the sapient Dr. Brown, who gave a certificate of insanity after a short conversation with her, and which certificate was to be used in aid of her incarceration for life —suffer as she has suffered, endure what she has endured, and the world would be deprived of future clinical revealings from his gigantic mind upon the subject of the spleen, and he would, to a still greater extent than in the past, "fail to illuminate" the public as to the virtues and glories of the martyr who is "watching and waiting" in Canada.

The heroic motto: "suffer and be strong," is fairly illustrated in her case. While many would have opposed force to his force, displayed frantic emotions of displeasure at such treatment, or sat convulsed and "maddened with the passion of her part," she meekly submitted to the tortures of her bigoted tormentor, trusting and believing in God's Providence the hour of her vindication and her release from thraldom would come. And now the fruit of her suffering and persecution has all the autumn glory of perfection

> "One who walked
> From the throne's splendor to the bloody block,
> Said: 'This completes my glory' with a smile
> Which still illuminates men's thoughts of her.'

Feeling the accusations of his guilty conscience, seeing the meshes of the net with which he had kept her surrounded were broken, and a storm-cloud of indignation about to break over his head in pitiless fury, the intolerant Packard, after encumbering their property with trust-deeds, and despoiling her of her furniture and clothing, left the country. Let him wander! with the mark of infamy upon his brow, through far-off States, where distance and obscurity may diminish till the grave shall cover the wrongs it cannot heal.

It is to be hoped Mrs. Packard will make immediate application for a divorce, and thereby relieve herself of a repetition of the wrongs and outrages she has suffered by him who for the past four years has only used the marriage relation to persecute and torment her in a merciless and unfeeling manner.

NARRATIVE OF EVENTS—CONTINUED.

When this Trial terminated, I returned to my home in Manteno, where five days previous I had bestowed the parting kiss upon my three youngest children, little thinking it would be the last embrace I should be allowed to bestow upon these dear objects of my warmest affections. But alas! so it proved to be. Mr. Packard had fled with them to Massachusetts, leaving me in the court room a childless widow. He could not but see that the tide of popular indignation was concentrating against him, as the revelations of the court ventilated the dreadful facts of this conspiracy, and he "fled his country," a fugitive from justice. He, however, left a letter for me which was handed me before I left the Court-house, wherein he stated that he had moved to Massachusetts, and extended to me an invitation to follow him, with the promise that he would provide me a suitable home. But I did not feel much like trusting either to his humanity or judgment in providing me another home. Indeed, I did not think it safe to follow him, knowing that Massachusetts' laws gave him the absolute custody of my person as well as Illinois' laws. He went to South Deerfield, Massachusetts, and sought shelter for himself and his children in the family of his sister, Mrs. Severance, one of his co-conspirators. Here he found willing ears to credit his tale of abuses he had suffered in this interference of his rights to do as he pleased with his lawful wife—and in representing the trial as a "mock trial," an illegal interference with his rights as head of his own household, and a "mob triumph,"—and in short, he was an innocent victim of a persecution against his legally constituted rights as a husband, to protect his wife in the way his own feelings of bigotry and intolerance should dictate!

This was the region of his nativity and former pastorate, which he had left about eleven years previously, with an unblemished external character, and sharing, to an uncommon degree, the entire confidence of the public as a Christian man and a minister. Nothing had occurred, *to their knowledge,* to disturb this confidence in his present integrity as an honest reporter, and the entire community credited his testimony as perfectly reliable, in his entire misrepresentations of the facts in the case, and the character of the trial. His view was, the only view the community were allowed to hear, so far as it was in his power to prevent it. The press also lent him its aid, as his organ of communication. He met also his old associates in the ministry, and by his artfully arranged web of lies, and his cunning sophistries, he deluded them also into a belief of his views, so that they, unanimously, gave him their certificate of confidence and fraternal sympathy. Yea, even my own father and brothers became victims also of his sophisms and misrepresentations, so that they honestly believed me to be insane, and that the Westerners had really interfered with Mr. Packard's rights and kind intents towards his wife, in intercepting as they had, his plans to keep her incarcerated for life.

Thus this one-sided view of the facts in the case so moulded public sentiment in this conservative part of New England, that he even obtained a certificate from my own dear father, a retired orthodox clergyman in Sunderland, Massachusetts, that, so far as he knew, he had treated his daughter generally with propriety!! This certificate served as a passport to the confidence of Sunderland people in Mr. Packard as a man and a minister, and procured for him a call to become their minister in holy things. He was accordingly hired, as stated supply, and paid fifteen dollars a Sabbath for one year and a half, and was boarded by my father in his family, part of the time, free of charge.

The condition in which Mr. Packard left me I will now give in the language of another, by inserting here a quotation from one of the many Chicago papers which published an account of this trial with editorial remarks accompanying it. The following is a part of one of these Editorial Articles, which appeared under the caption:—

"A HEARTLESS CLERGYMAN."

Chicago, March 6, 1864.

"We recently gave an extended account of the melancholy case of Mrs. Packard, of Manteno, Ill., and showed how she was persecuted by her husband, Rev. Theophilus Packard, a bigoted Presbyterian minister of Manteno. Mrs. Packard became liberal in her views, in fact, avowed Universalist sentiments; and as her husband was unable to answer her arguments, he thought he could silence her tongue, by calling her *insane,* and having her incarcerated in the Insane Asylum at Jacksonville, Illinois. He finally succeeded in finding one or two orthodox physicians, as bigoted as himself, ready to aid him in his nefarious work, and she was confined in the asylum, under the charge (?) of Dr. Mc Farland, who kept her there three years. She at last succeeded in having a jury trial, and was pronounced *sane*. Previous, however, to the termination of the trial, this persecutor of his wife, mortgaged his property, took away his children from the mother, and left her penniless and homeless, without a cent to buy food, or a place where to lay her head! And yet he pretended to believe that she was *insane!* Is this the way to treat an insane wife! Abandon her, turn her out upon the world without a morsel of bread, and no home? Her husband calls her *insane*. Before the case is decided by the jury, he starts for parts unknown. Was there ever such a case of heartlessness? If Mr. Packard *believed* his wife to be hopelessly *insane*, why did he abandon her? Is this the way to treat a companion afflicted with insanity? If he believed his own story, he should, like a devoted husband, have watched over her with tenderness, his heart full of love should have gone out towards the poor, afflicted woman, and he should have bent over her and soothed her, and spent the last penny he had, for her recovery! But instead of this, he gathers in his funds, "packs up his duds," and leaves his poor, *insane* wife, as *he* calls her, in the court room, without food or shelter. He abandons her, leaving her penniless, homeless and childless!

"Mrs. Packard is now residing with Mr. Z. Handford, of Manteno, who writes to the Kankakee *Gazette* as follows:

"In the first place, Mrs. Packard is now penniless. After having aided her husband for twenty-one years, by her most indefatigable exertions, to secure for themselves a home, with all its clustering comforts, he, with no cause, except a difference in religious opinions, exiled her from her home, by forcing her into Jacksonville Insane Asylum, where he hoped to immure her for life, or until she would abandon what *he* calls her 'insane notions.'

"But in the overruling providence of a just God, her case has been ventilated, at last, by a jury trial, the account of which is already before the public.

"From the time of her banishment into exile, now more than three and a half years, he has not allowed her the control of one dollar of their personal property. And she has had nothing to do with their real estate, within that time, excepting to sign one deed for the transfer of some of their real estate in Mount Pleasant, Iowa, which she did at her husband's earnest solicitations, and his promise to let her have her 'defense,' long enough to copy, which document he had robbed her of three years before, by means of Dr. McFarland as agent. Her signature, *thus obtained*, was acknowledged as a valid act, and the deed was presented to the purchaser as a valid instrument, even after Mr. Packard had just before taken an *oath* that his wife was an *insane* woman!

"He has robbed her of all her patrimony, including not only her furniture, but her valuable clothing also, and a note of six hundred dollars on interest, which he gave her seven years before, as an equivalent for this amount of patrimony which her father, Rev. Samuel Ware, of Sunderland, Massachusetts, sent Mrs. Packard for her special benefit, and to be used for her and her children as her own judgment should dictate. He has taken her furniture and clothing, or the avails of them, with him to Massachusetts, without allowing her a single article of furniture for her own individual comfort and use. Thus he has left her without a single penny of their common property to procure for herself the necessaries of life.

"He has left her homeless. Before the court closed, Mr. Packard left this scene of revelations, and mortgaged and rented their home in Manteno, and dispossessed it by night of its furniture, so that when the court closed, Mrs. Packard had no sort of home to return to, the new renter having claimed possession of her home, and claiming a legal right to all its privileges, excluding her from its use entirely as a home, without leaving her the least legal claim to any of the avails of the rent or sales for the supply of her present necessities.

"Again, she is childless. Her cruel husband, not satisfied with robbing his wife of all her rightful property, has actually *kidnapped* all her dear children who lived at home, taking them with him, clandestinely, to Massachusetts, leaving her a 'childless widow,' entirely dependent for her living, either upon her own exertions, or the charities of the public. We will not attempt to describe the desolation of her maternal heart, when she returned to her deserted home, to find it despoiled of all her dearest earthly treasures; with no sweet cherub, with its smiling, joyous face to extend to her the happy, welcome kiss of a mother's return.

"But one short week previous, Mrs. Packard had bestowed the parting kiss upon her three youngest children, little dreaming it would be the last embrace the mother would ever be allowed to bestow upon her dear offspring, in their own dear home. But now, alas! where is her only daughter, Elizabeth, of thirteen years, and her George Hastings, of ten years, and her darling baby, Arthur Dwight, of five years? Gone! gone! never to return, while the mandate of their father's iron will usurps supreme control of this household!

"Yes, the mother's home and heart are both desolate, for her heart-treasures—her dear children—are no more to be found. At length, rumor reaches her that her babe, Arthur, is at their brother Dole's. The anxious mother hastens to seek for it there. But all in vain. The family, faithful to their brother's wishes, keep the babe carefully hid from the mother, so that she cannot get even one glimpse of her sweet, darling boy. Her cruel husband, fearing her attempts to secure the child might prove successful, has sent for it to be brought to him in Massachusetts, where he now is fairly out of the mother's reach.'" Z. HANFORD.

I made various attempts to recover my furniture, which I found was stored at Deacon Doles' house, a brother-in-law of Mr. Packard's, under the pretense, that he had bought it, although he could never show one paper as proof of property transferred. I took counsel of the Judge and lawyers at Kankakee, to see if I could in any way recover my stolen furniture, which I had bought with my own patrimony. "Can I replevy it as stolen property?" said I. "No," said my advisers, "you cannot replevy anything, for you are a married woman, and a married woman has no legal existence, unless she holds property independent of her husband. As this is not your case, you are nothing and nobody in law. Your husband has a legal right to all your common property—you have not even a right to the hat on your head!" "Why?" said I, "I have bought and paid for it with my own money." "That is of no consequence—you can hold nothing, as you are *nothing and nobody* in law! You have a moral right to your own things, and your own children, but no legal right at all; therefore you, a married woman, cannot replevy, although any one else could under like circumstances." "Is this so? Has a married woman no identity in Statute Book of Illinois?" "It is so. Her interests are all lost in those of her husband, and he has the absolute control of her home, her property, her children, and her personal liberty."

Yes, all this is but too true, as my own sad experience fully demonstrates. Now I can realize the sad truths so often iterated, reiterated to me by my husband, namely: "You have no *right* to your home, I have let you live with me twenty-one years in my home as a favor to you. You have no *right* to your children. I let you train them, as far as I think it is proper to trust your judgment—this privilege of training and educating your own children is a favor bestowed upon you by me, which I can withold or grant at my own option. You have no *right* to your money patrimony after you intrusted it to my care, and I gave you a note for it on interest which I can either pay you or not at my own option. You have no *right* to your personal liberty if I feel disposed to christen your opinions insane opinions, for I can then treat you as an insane person or not, just at my own option." Yes, Mr. Packard has only treated me as he said the laws of Illinois allowed him to do, and how can he be blamed then? Did not "wise men" make the laws, as he often used to assert they did? And can one be prosecuted for doing a legal act? Nay—verily—no law can reach him; even his kidnapping me as he did is legalized in Illinois Statute Book, as the following article which was published in several Boston papers in the winter of 1865, demonstrates, namely:

"LEGAL KIDNAPPING," OR PROVISION FOR A SANE PERSON'S IMPRISONMENT.

"From the 'Disclosures' of Mrs. Packard's book, it appears a self-evident fact that one State of our Union has an express provision for the imprisonment of married women who are not insane. And this process of legal kidnapping is most strikingly illustrated in the facts developed in Mrs. Packard's own experience, as delineated in her book entitled 'The Great Drama.'

"The following is a copy of the Law, as it now stands on the Illinois Statute Book:—

"AMENDATORY ACT."
"Session Laws 15, 1851. Page 96."

"Sec. 10. Married women and infants who, in the judgment of the Medical Superintendent, [meaning the Superintendent of the 'Illinois State Hospital" for the insane] are evidently insane or distracted, may be entered or detained in the Hospital on the request of the husband, or the woman or guardian of the infants, *without* the evidence of insanity required in other cases."

"Hon. S. S. Jones of St. Charles, Illinois, thus remarks upon this Act:—

"Thus we see a corrupt husband, with money enough to corrupt a Superintendent, can get rid of a wife as effectually as was ever done in a more barbarous age. The Superintendent may be corrupted either with money or influence, that he thinks will give him position, place, or emoluments. Is not this a pretty statute to be incorporated into our laws no more than thirteen years ago? Why not confine the husband at the instance of the wife, as well as the wife at the instance of the husband? The wife evidently had no voice in making the law.

"Who, being a man, and seeing this section in the Statute Book of Illinois, under the general head of 'Charities,' does not blush and hang his head for very shame at legislative perversion of so holy a term? I have no doubt, if the truth of the matter were known, this act was passed at the special instance of the Superintendent. A desire for power. I do not know why it has not been noted by me and others before."

"And we would also venture to inquire, what is the married woman's protection under such a Statute law? Is she not allowed counter testimony from a physician of her own choice, or can she not demand a trial of some kind, to show whether the charge of insanity brought against her is true or false? Nay, verily. The Statute expressly states that the judgment of the medical Superintendent, to whom the husband's request is made, is *all* that is required for him to incarcerate his wife for any indefinite period of time. Neither she, her children, nor her relatives have any voice at all in the matter. Her imprisonment may be life-long, for anything she or her friends can do for her to prevent it. If the husband has money or influence enough to corrupt the officials, he can carry out his single wishes concerning his wife's life-destiny.

"Are not the 'Divorce Laws' of Illinois made a necessity, o meet the demands of the wife, as her only refuge from this exposure to a 'false imprisonment' for life in an Insane Asylum?

"We hope our readers will be able to read Mrs. Packard's book for themselves; especially her 'Self-defence from the charge of Insanity,' wherein the barbarities of this statute are made to appear in their true light, as being merely a provision for 'Legal Kidnapping.'"

BOSTON, Feb. 24, 1865.

Satisfied as I was that there was no legal redress for me in the laws, and no hope in appealing to Mr. Packard's mercy or manliness, I determined to do what I could to obtain a self-reliant position, by securing if possible the protection of greenbacks, confident that this kind of protection is better than none at all. I concluded, therefore, to publish the first installment of "The Great Drama," an allegorical book I wrote while in the Asylum, consisting of twelve parts. But how could this be done in my penniless condition? was the great question to be practically settled. I accordingly borrowed ten dollars of Mr. Z. Hanford, of Manteno, a noble, kind hearted man, who offered me a home at his house after the trial, and went to Chicago to consult the printers in reference to the expense of printing one thousand copies of this book, and get it stereotyped. I found it would cost me five hundred dollars. I then procured a few thousand tickets on which was printed—"The bearer is entitled to the first volume of Mrs. Packard's book, entitled the Great Drama. None are genuine without my signature. Mrs. E. P. W. Packard." And commenced canvassing for my unborn book, by selling these tickets for fifty cents each, assuring the purchaser I would redeem the ticket in three month's time, by giving them a book worth fifty cents. When I had sold about eight or nine hundred tickets, I went to Chicago to set my printers and stereotypers, engravers and binders, at work on my book. But I now met with a new and unlooked for difficulty, in the sudden inflation of prices in labor and material. My book could not now be printed for less than seven hundred dollars; so that my first edition would not pay for itself into two hundred dollars. As the case now was, instead of paying for my book by selling one thousand tickets, I must sell fourteen hundred, besides superintending the various workmen on the different departments of my book. Nothing daunted by this reverse, instead of raising the price of my tickets to seventy-five cents to meet this unfortunate turn in my finances, I found I must fall back upon the only sure guarantee of success, namely: patient perseverance. By the practical use of this great backbone of success, perseverance, I did finally succeed in printing my book, and paying the whole seven hundred dollars for it in three months' time, by selling four hundred tickets in advance on another edition. I sold and printed, and then printed and sold, and so on, until I have printed and sold in all, twelve thousand books in fifteen months' time. Included in this twelve thousand are several editions of smaller pamphlets, varying in price from five to twenty-five cents each.

INTERVIEW WITH MAYOR SHERMAN.

At this stage of my Narrative it may not be inappropriate to narrate my interview with Mayor Sherman, of Chicago, since it not only discloses one of the dangers and the difficulties I had to encounter, in prosecuting my enterprise, but also serves as another exemplification of that marital power which is legally guaranteed to the husband, leaving the wife utterly helpless, and legally defenceless.

I called upon him at his office in the court house, and was received with respectful, manly courtesy. After introducing myself as the Mrs. Packard whose case had recently acquired so much notoriety through the Chicago press, and after briefly recapitulating the main facts of the persecution, I said to him:

"Now, Mr. Sherman, as the Mayor of this city, I appeal to you for protection, while printing my book in your city. Will you protect me here?"

"Why, Mrs. Packard, what protection do you need? What dangers do you apprehend?"

"Sir, I am a married woman, and my husband is my persecutor, therefore I have no legal protection. The husband is, you probably know, the wife's only protector in the law, therefore, what I want now, Sir, is protection against my protector!"

"Is he in this city?"

"No, Sir; but his agents are, and he can delegate his power to them, and authorize them what to do."

"What do you fear he will do?"

"I fear he may intercept the publication of my book; for you probably know, Sir, he can come either himself, or by proxy, and, with his Sheriff, can demand my mannscript of my printer, and the printer, nor you, Sir, have no legal power to defend it. He can demand it, and burn it, and I am helpless in legal self-defense. For, Sir, my identity was legally lost in his, when I married him, leaving me nothing and nobody in law; and besides, all I have is his in law, and of course no one can prosecute him for taking his own things—my manuscript is his, and entirely at his disposal. I have no right in law even to my own thoughts, either spoken or written—he has even claimed the right to superintend my written thoughts as well as post office rights. I can not claim these rights—they are mine only as he grants me them as his gifts to me."

"What does your printer say about it?"

"He says if the Sheriff comes to him for the book he shall tell him he must get the book where he can find it; *I* shall not find it for him. I then said to my printer, supposing he should come with money, and offer to buy the manuscript, what then?" "I say, it will take more money than there is in Chicago to buy that manuscript of us," replied my printer.

"I think that sounds like protection, Mrs. Packard. I think you have nothing to fear."

"No, Mr. Sherman, I have nothing to fear from the manliness of my printer, for this is my sole and only protection—but as one man to whom I trusted even myself, has proved a traitor to his manliness, is there not a possibility another may. I should not object to a double guard, since the single guard of manliness has not even protected me from imprisonment."

"Well, Mrs. Packard, you shall have my protection; and I can also assure you the protection of my counsel, also. If you get into trouble, apply to us, and we will give you all the help the laws will allow."

"I beg you to consider, Sir, the laws do not allow you to interfere in such a matter. Are you authorized to stop a man from doing a *legal* act?"

"No, Mrs. Packard, I am not. I see you are without any legal protection. Still I think you are safe in Chicago."

"I hope it may so prove, Sir. But one thing more I wish your advice about; how can I keep the money I get for my book from Mr. Packard, the legal owner of it?"

"Keep it about your person, so he can't get it."

"But, Sir; Mr. Packard has a right to my person in law, and can take it anywhere, and put it where he pleases; and if he can get my person, he can take what is on it."

"That's so—you are in a bad case, truly—I must say, I never before knew that any one under our government was so utterly defenceless as you are. Your case ought to be known. Every soldier in our army ought to have one of your books, so as to have our laws changed."

Soldiers of our army! receive this tacit compliment from Mayor Sherman. *You* are henceforth to hold the reins of the American Government. And it is my candid opinion, they could not be in better or safer hands. And in your hands would I most confidently trust my sacred cause—the cause of Married Woman; for, so far as my observation extends, no class of American citizens are more manly, than our soldiers. I am inclined to cherish the idea, that gallantry and patriotism are identified; at least, I find they are almost always associated together in the same manly heart.

When I had sold about half of my twelve thousand books, I resolved to visit my relatives in Massachusetts, who had not seen me for about twelve years. I felt assured that my dear father, and brothers, and my kind step-mother, were all looking at the facts of my persecution from a wrong stand-point; and I determined to risk my exposure to Mr. Packard's persecuting power again, so far as to let my relatives see me once for themselves; hoping thus the scales might drop from their eyes, so far at least as to protect me from another kidnapping from Mr. Packard

I arrived first at my brother Austin Ware's house in South Deerfield, who lives about two miles from Mr. Severance, where were my three youngest children, and where Mr. Packard spent one day of each week. I spent two nights with him and his new wife, who both gave me a very kind and patient hearing; and the result was, their eyes were opened to see their error in believing me to be an insane person, and expressed their decided condemnation of the course Mr. Packard had pursued towards me. Brother became at once my gallant and manly protector, and the defender of my rights. "Sister," said he, "you have a right to see your children, and you shall see them. I will send for them to-day." He accordingly sent a team for them twice, but was twice refused by Mr. Packard, who had heard of my arrival. Still, he assured me I should see them in due time. He carried me over to Sunderland, about four miles distant, to my father's house, promising me I should meet my dear children there; feeling confident that my father's request joined with his own, would induce Mr. Packard to let me see once more my own dear offspring. As he expected, my father at once espoused my cause, and assured me I should see my children; "for," added he, "Mr. Packard knows it will not do for him to refuse me." He then directed brother to go directly for them himself, and say to Mr. Packard: "Elizabeth's father requests him to let the children have an interview with their mother at his house." But, instead of the children, came a letter from brother, saying, that Mr. Packard has refused, in the most decided terms, to let sister see her own children; or, to use his own language, he said, "I came from Illinois to Massachusets to protect the children from their mother, and I shall do it, in spite of you, or father Ware, or any one else!" Brother adds, "the mystery of this dark case is now solved, in my mind, completely. Mr. Packard is a monomaniac on this subject; there is no more reason in his treatment of sister, than in a brute."

These facts of his refusal to let me see my children, were soon in circulation in the two adjacent villages of Sunderland and South Deerfield, and a strongly indignant feeling was manifested against Mr. Packard's defiant and unreasonable position; and he, becoming aware of the danger to his interests which a conflict with this tide of public sentiment might occasion, seemed forced, by this pressure of public opinion, to succumb; for, on the following Monday morning, (this was on Saturday, P. M.,) he brought all of my three children to my father's house, with himself and Mrs. Severance, as their body-guard, and with both as my witnesses, I was allowed to talk with them an hour or two. He refused me an interview with them alone in my room.

I remained at my father's house a few days only, knowing that even in Massachusetts the laws did not protect me from another similar outrage, if Mr. Packard could procure the certificate of two physicians that I was insane; for, with these alone, without any chance at self-defense, he could force me into some of the Private Asylums here, as he did into a State Asylum in Illinois.

I knew that, as I was Mr. Packard's wife, neither my brother nor father could be my legal protectors in such an event, as they could command no influence in my defense, except that of public sentiment or mob-law. I therefore felt forced to leave my father's house in self-defence, to seek some protection of the Legislature of Massachusetts, by petitioning them for a change in their laws on the mode of commitment into Insane Asylums. As a preparatory step, I endeavored to get up an agitation on the subject, by printing and selling about six thousand books relative to the subject; and then, trusting to this enlightened public sentiment to back up the movement, I petitioned Massachusetts Legislature to make the needed change in the laws. Hon. S. E. Sewall, of Boston, drafted the Petition, and I circulated it, and obtained between one and two hundred names of men of the first standing and influence in Boston, such as the Aldermen, the Common Council, the High Sheriff, and several other City Officers; and besides, Judges, Lawyers, Editors, Bank Directors, Physicians, &c. Mr. Sewall presented this petition to the Legislature, and they referred it to a committee, and this committee had seven special meetings on the subject. I was invited to meet with them each time, and did so, as were also Mrs. Phelps and Mrs. Denny, two ladies of Boston who had suffered a term of false imprisonment in a private institution at Sommersville, without any previous trial. Hon. S. E. Sewall and Mr. Wendell Phillips both made a plea in its behalf before this committee, and the gallantry and manliness of this committee allowed me a hearing of several hour's time in all, besides allowing me to present the two following Bills, which they afterwards requested a copy of in writing. The three Superintendents, Dr. Walker, Dr. Jarvis, and Dr. Tyler, represented the opposition. And my reply to Dr. Walker constituted the preamble to my bills.

MRS. PACKARD'S BILLS.

PREAMBLE.

Gentlemen of the Committee:

I feel it my duty to say one word in defence of the Petitioners, in reply to Dr. Walker's statement, that, "in his opinion, nineteen twentieths of the petitioners did not know nor care what they petitioned for, and that they signed it out of compliment to the lady."

I differ from Dr. Walker in opinion on this point, for this reason. I obtained these names by my own individual appeals, except from most of the members of the "Common Council," who signed it during an evening session, by its being passed around for their names. I witnessed their signing, and saw them read it, carefully, before signing it. And I *think* they signed it intelligently, and from a desire for safer legislation. The others I *know* signed intelligently, and for this reason. And I could easily have got one thousand more names, had it been necessary; for, in selling my books, I have conversed with many thousand men on this subject, and among them all, I have only found one man who defends the present mode of commitment, by leaving it all to the physicians.

I spent a day in the Custom House, and a day and a half in the Navy Yard, and these men, like all others, defend our movement. I have sold one hundred and thirty-nine books in the Navy Yard within the last day and a half, by conversing personally with gentlemen in their counting-rooms on this subject, and they are carefully watching your decision on this question.

Now, from this stand-point of extensive observation, added to my own personal experience, I feel fully confident these two Bills are needed to meet the public demand at this crisis.

Bill No. 1.

No person shall be regarded or treated as an Insane person, or a Monomaniac, simply for the *expression of opinions*, no matter how absurd these opinions may appear to others.

REASONS.

1st. This Law is needed for the personal safety of Reformers. We are living in a Progressive Age. Everything is in a state of transmutation, and, as our laws now are, the Reformer, the Pioneer, the Originator of any new idea is liable to be treated as a Monomaniac, with *imprisonment*.

2d. It is a *Crime* against human progress to allow Reformers to be treated as Monomaniacs; for, who will dare to be true to the inspirations of the divinity within them, if the Pioneers of truth are thus liable to lose their personal liberty for life by so doing?

3d. It is *Treason* against the principles of our Government to treat opinions as Insanity, and to imprison for it, as our present laws allow.

4th. There always are those in every age who are opposed to every thing *new*, and if allowed, will persecute Reformers with the stigma of Insanity. This has been the fate of all Reformers, from the days of Christ—the Great Reformer—until the present age.

5th. Our Government, of all others, ought especially to guard, by legislation, the vital principle on which it is based, namely: *individuality*, which guarantees an individual right of opinion to all persons.

Therefore, gentlemen, *protect your thinkers!* by a law, against the charge of Monomania, and posterity shall bless our government, as a model government, and Massachusetts as the Pioneer State, in thus protecting individuality as the vital principle on which the highest development of humanity rests.

Bill No. 2.

No person shall be imprisoned, and treated as an insane person, except for *irregularities of conduct*, such as indicate that the individual is so lost to reason, as to render him an unaccountable moral agent.

REASONS.

Multitudes are now imprisoned, without the least evidence that reason is dethroned, as indicated by this test. And I am a representative of this class of prisoners; for, when Dr. McFarland was driven to give his reasons for regarding me as insane, on *this* basis, the only reason which he could name, after closely inspecting my conduct for three years, was, that I once "*fell down stairs!*"

I do insist upon it, gentlemen, that no person should be imprisoned without a *just cause;* for personal liberty is the most blessed boon of our existence. and ought therefore to be reasonably guarded as an inalienable right. But it is *not* reasonably protected under our present legislation, while it allows the simple *opinion* of two doctors to imprison a person for life, without one *proof* in the *conduct* of the accused, that he is an unaccountable moral agent. We do not hang a person on the simple *opinion* that he is a murderer, but *proof* is required from the accused's *own actions,* that he is guilty'of the charge which forfeits his life. So the charge which forfeits our personal liberty ought to be *proved* from the individual's own conduct, before imprisonment.

So long as insanity is treated as a *crime*, instead of a *misfortune*, as our present system *practically* does so treat it, the protection of our individual liberty imperatively demands such an enactment. Many contend that *every* person is insane on some point. On this ground, *all* persons are liable to be legally imprisoned, under our present system; for intelligent physicians are everywhere to be found, who will not scruple to give a certificate that an individual is a Monomaniac on *that* point where he differs from *him* in opinion! This Monomania in many instances is not Insanity, but individuality, which is the highest *natural* development of a human being.

·Gentlemen, I know, and have felt, the horrors—the untold *soul* agonies—attendant on such a persecution. Therefore, as Philanthropists, I beg of you to guard your own liberties, and those of your countrymen, by recommending the adoption of these two Bills as an imperative necessity.

The above Bills were presented to the Committee on the Commitment of the Insane, in Boston State House, March 29, 1865, by

Mrs. E. P. W. Packard.

The result was, the petition triumphed, by so changing the mode of commitment, that, instead of the husband being allowed to enter his wife at his simple request, added to the certificate of two physicians, he must now get ten of her nearest relatives to join with him in this request; and the person committed, instead of not being allowed to communicate by writing to any one outside of the Institution, except under the censorship of the Superintendent, can now send a letter to each of these ten relatives, and to any other two persons whom the person committed shall designate. This the Superintendent is required to do within two days from the time of commitment.

This Law is found in Chapter 268, Section 2, of the General Laws of Massachusetts. I regard my personal liberty in Massachusetts now as not absolutely in the power of my husband; as my family friends must now co-operate in order to make my commitment legal. And since my family relatives are now fully satisfied of my sanity, after having seen me for themselves, I feel now comparatively safe, while in Massachusetts. I therefore returned to my father's house in Sunderland, and finding both of my dear parents feeble, and in need of some one to care for them, and finding myself in need of a season of rest and quiet, I accepted their kind invitation to make their house my home for the present. At this point my father indicated his true position in relation to my interests, by his self-moved efforts in my behalf, in writing and sending the following letter to Mr. Packard.*

COPY OF FATHER WARE'S LETTER TO MR. PACKARD.

"*Sunderland, Sept.* 2, 1865.

"REV. SIR: I think the time has fully come for you to give up to Elizabeth her clothes. Whatever reason might have existed to justify you in retaining them, has, in process of time, entirely vanished. There is not a shadow of excuse for retaining them. It is my presumption there is not an individual in this town who would justify you in retaining them a single day. Elizabeth is about to make a home at my house, and I must be her protector. She is very destitute of clothing, and greatly needs all those articles which are hers. I hope to hear from you soon, before I shall be constrained to take another step. Yours, Respectfully,

"REV. T. PACKARD.   SAMUEL WARE."

The result of this letter was, that in about twenty-four hours after the letter was delivered, Mr. Packard brought the greater part of my wardrobe and delivered it into the hands of my father.

In a few weeks after this event, Mr. Packard's place in the pulpit in Sunderland was filled by a candidate for settlement, and he left the place. The reasons why he thus left his ministerial charge in this place, cannot perhaps be more summarily given than by transcribing

* See Appendix, p. 138.

the following letter which father got me to write for him, in answer to Rev. Dr. Pomeroy's letter, inquiring of my father *why* Mr. Packard had left Sunderland.

LETTER TO REV. DR. POMEROY.

Sunderland, Oct. 28, 1865.

Dr. Pomeroy, Dear Sir: I am sorry to say that my dear father feels too weak to reply to your kind and affectionate letter of the twenty-third instant, and therefore I cheerfully consent to reply to it myself.

As to the subject of your letter, it is as you intimated. We have every reason to believe that father's defence of me, has been the indirect cause of Mr. Packard's leaving Sunderland; although we knew nothing of the matter until he left, and a candidate filled his place. Neither father, mother, nor I, have used any direct influence to undermine the confidence of this people in Mr. Packard. But where this simple fact, that I have been imprisoned three years, is known, to have become a demonstrated truth, by the decision of a jury, after a thorough legal investigation of five day's trial, it is found to be rather of an unfortunate truth for the public sentiment of the present age to grapple with. And Mr. Packard and his persecuting party may yet find I uttered no fictitious sentiment, when I remarked to Dr. McFarland in the Asylum, that I shall yet *live down* this slander of Insanity, and also live down my persecutors. And Mr. Packard is affording me every facility for so doing, by his continuing strenuously to insist upon it, that I am, now, just as insane as when he incarcerated me in Jacksonville Insane Asylum. And he still insists upon it, that an Asylum Prison is the only suitable place for me to spend the residue of my earth-life in. But, fortunately for me, my friends judge differently upon seeing me for themselves. Especially fortunate is it for me, that my own dear father feels confident that his house is a more suitable home for me, notwithstanding the assertion of Mrs. Dickinson, (the widow with whom Mr. Packard boards,) that, "it is such a pity that Mrs. Packard should come to Sunderland, where Mr. Packard preaches!" Mr. Johnson replied in answer to this remark, that he thought Mrs. Packard had a right to come to her father's house for protection, and also that her father had an equal right to extend protection to his only daughter, when thrown adrift and pennyless upon the cold world without a place to shelter her defenceless head.

Mr. Packard has withdrawn all intercourse with us all since he was called upon by father to return my wardrobe to me. Would that Mr. Packard's eyes might be opened to see what he is doing, and repent, so that I might be allowed to extend to him the forgiveness my heart longs to bestow, upon this gospel condition.

Thankful for all the kindness and sympathy you have bestowed upon my father and mother, as well as myself, I subscribe myself your true friend, E. P. W. PACKARD.

P. S. Father and mother both approve of the above, which I have written at father's urgent request. E. P. W. P.

Fidelity to the truth requires me to add one more melancholy fact, in order to make this narrative of events complete, and that is, that Mr. Packard has made merchandise of this stigma of Insanity he has branded me with, and used it as a lucrative source of gain to himself, in the following manner. He has made most pathetic appeals to the sympathies of the public for their charities to be bestowed upon him, on the plea of his great misfortune in having an insane wife to support—one who was incapable of taking care of herself or her six children—and on this false premise he has based a most pathetic argument and appeal to their sympathies for pecuniary help, in the form of boxes of clothing for himself and his destitute and defenceless children. These appeals have been most generously responded to from the American Home Missionary Society. So that when I returned to my home from the Asylum, I counted twelve boxes of such clothing, some of which were very large, containing the spoils he had thus purloined from this benevolent society, by entirely false representations.

My family were not destitute. But on the contrary, were abundantly supplied with a supernumerary amount of such missionary gifts, which had been lavished upon us, at his request, before I was imprisoned. I had often said to him, that I and my children had already more than a supply for our wants until they were grown up. Now, what could he do with twelve more such boxes? My son, Isaac, now in Chicago, and twenty-one years of age, told me he had counted fifty new vests in one pile, and he had as many pants and coats, and overcoats, and almost every thing else, of men's wearing apparel, in like ratio. He said I had a pile of dress patterns accumulated from these boxes, to one yard in depth in one solid pile. And this was only one sample of all kinds of ladies' apparel which he had thus accumulated, by his cunningly devised begging system.

Still, to this very date, he is pleading want and destitution as a basis for more charities of like kind. He has even so moved the benevolent sympathies of the widow Dickinson with whom he boarded, as to make her feel that he was an honest claimant upon their charities in this line, on the ground of poverty and destitution. She accordingly started a subscription to procure him a suit of clothes, on the ground of his extreme destitution, and finally succeeded in begging a subscription of one hundred and thirteen dollars for his benefit, and presented it to him as a token of sympathy and regard.

Another fact, he has put his property out of his hands, so that he can say he has nothing. And should I sue him for my maintainance, I could get nothing. His rich brother-in-law, George Hastings, supports the three youngest children, mostly, thus leaving scarcely no claimants upon his own purse, except his own personal wants. His wife and six children he has so disposed of, as to be almost entirely independent of him of any support. And it is my honest opinion, that had Sunderland people known of these facts in his financial matters, they would not have presented him with one hundred and thirteen dollars, as a token of their sympathy and esteem. Still, looking at the subject from their stand-point, I have no doubt they acted conscientiously in this matter. I have never deemed it my duty to enlighten them on this subject, except as the truth is sought for from me, in a few individual isolated cases. I do not mingle with the people scarcely at all, and have sold none of my books among them. Self-defence does not require me to seek the protection of enlightened public sentiment now that the laws protect my personal liberty, while in Massachusetts.

But fidelity to the cause of humanity, especially the cause of "Married Woman," requires me to make public the facts of this notorious persecution, in order to have her true legal position known and fully apprehended. And since my case is a practical illustration of what the law is on this subject—showing how entirely destitute she is of any legal protection, except what the will and wishes of her husband secures to her—and also demonstrates the fact, that the common-law, everywhere, in relation to married woman, not only gravitates towards an absolute despotism, but even protects and sustains and defends a despotism of the most arbitrary and absolute kind. Therefore, in order to have her social position changed legally, the need of this change must first be seen and appreciated by the common people—the law-makers of this Republic. And this need or necessity for a revolution on this subject can be made to appear in no more direct manner, than by a practical case, such as my own furnishes. As the need of a revolution of the law in relation to negro servitude was made to appear, by the practical exhibition of the Slave Code in "Uncle Tom's" experience, showing that all slaves were *liable* to suffer to the extent he did; so my experience, although like "Uncle Tom's," an extreme case, shows how all married women are *liable* to suffer to the same extent that I have. Now justice to humanity claims that such liabilities should not exist in any Christian government. The laws should be so changed that such another outrage could not possibly take place under the sanction of the laws of a Christian government.

As Uncle Tom's case aroused the indignation of the people against the slave code, so my case, so far as it is known, arouses this same feeling of indignation against those laws which protect married servitude. Married woman needs legal emancipation from married servitude, as much as the slave needed legal emancipation from his servitude.

Again, all slaves did not suffer under negro slavery, neither do all married women suffer from this legalized servitude. Still, the principle of slavery is wrong, and the principle of emancipation is right, and the laws ought so to regard it. And this married servitude exposes the wife to as great suffering as negro servitude did. It is my candid opinion, that no Southern slave ever suffered more spiritual agony than I have suffered; as I am more developed in my moral and spiritual nature than they are, therefore more capable of suffering. I think no slave mother ever endured more keen anguish by being deprived of her own offspring than I have in being legally separated from mine. God grant, that married woman's emancipation may quickly follow in the wake of negro emancipation!

MISCELLANEOUS QUESTIONS ANSWERED.

In canvassing for my books various important questions have been propounded to me, which the preceding Narrative of Events does not fully answer.

First Question.

"Why, Mrs. Packard, do you not get a divorce?"

Because, in the first place, I do not want to be a divorced woman; but, on the contrary, I wish to be a married woman, and have my husband for my protector; for I do not like this being divorced from my own home. I want a home to live in, and I prefer the one I have labored twenty one years myself to procure, and furnished to my own taste and mind. Neither do I like this being divorced from my own children. I want to live with my dear children, whom I have borne and nursed, reared and educated, almost entirely by my own unwearied indefatigable exertions; and I love them, with all the fondness of a mother's undying love, and no place is home to me in this wide world without them. And again, I have done nothing to *deserve* this exclusion from the rights and privileges of my own dear home; but on the contrary, my untiring fidelity to the best interests of my family for twenty-one years of healthful, constant service, having never been sick during this time so as to require five dollars doctor's bill to be paid for me or my six children, and having done all the housework, sewing, nursing, and so forth, of my entire family for twenty-one years, with no hired girl help, except for only nine months, during all this long period of constant toil and labor. I say, this self-sacrificing devotion to the best interests of my family and home, deserve and claim a right to be protected in it, at least, so long as my good conduct continues, instead of being divorced from it, against my own will or consent. In short, what I want is, *protection in my home*, instead of a divorce from it. I do not wish to drive Mr. Packard from his own home, and exclude him from all its rights and privileges—neither do I want he should treat me in this manner, especially so long as he himself claims that I have *always* been a most kind, patient, devoted wife and mother. He even claims as his justification of his course, that I am so *good* a woman, and he *loves* me so well, that he wants to save me from fatal errors!

It is my opinions—my religious opinions—and those alone, he makes an occasion for treating me as he has. He frankly owned to me, that he was putting me into an Asylum so that my reputation for being an insane person might destroy the influence of my religious opinions; and I see in one letter which he wrote to my father, he mentions this as the chief evidence of my insanity. He writes: "Her many excellences and past services I highly appreciate; but she says she has widely departed from, or progressed beyond, her former religious views and sentiments—and I think it is too true!!" Here is all the insanity he claims, or has attempted to prove.

Now comes the question: Is this a crime for which I ought to be divorced from all the comforts and privileges of my own dear home?

To do this,—that is, to get a divorce—would it not be becoming an accomplice in crime, by doing the very deed which he is so desirous of having done, namely: to remove me from my family, for fear of the contaminating influence of my new views? Has a married woman no rights at all? Can she not even think her own thoughts, and speak her own words, unless her thoughts and expressions harmonize with those of her husband? I think it is high time the merits of this question should be practically tested, on a proper basis, the basis of truth—of facts. And the fact, that I have been not only practically divorced from my own home and children, but also incarcerated for three years in a prison, simply for my religious belief, by the arbitrary will of my husband, ought to raise the question, as to what are the married woman's rights, and what is her protection? And it is to this practical issue I have ever striven to force this question. And this issue I felt might be reached more directly and promptly by the public mind, by laying the necessities of the case before the community, and by a direct appeal to them for personal protection—instead of getting a divorce for my protection. I know that by so doing, I have run a great risk of losing my liberty again. Still, I felt that the great cause of married woman's rights might be promoted by this agitation; and so far as my own feelings were concerned, I felt willing to suffer even another martyrdom in this cause, if so be, my sisters in the bonds of marital power might be benefited thereby.

I want and seek protection, *as a married woman*—not divorce, in order to escape the abuses of marital power—that is, I want protection from the abuse of marital power, not a divorce from it. I can live in my home with my husband, if he will only let me do so; but he will not suffer it, unless I recant my religious belief. Cannot religious bigotry under such manifestations, receive *some* check under our government, which is professedly based on the very principle of religious tolerance to all? Cannot there be laws enacted by which a married woman can stand on the same platform as a married man— that is, have an equal right, at least, to the protection of her inalienable rights? And is not this our petition for protection founded in justice and humanity?

Is it just to leave the weakest and most defenceless of these two parties wholly without the shelter of law to shield her, while the strongest and most independent has all the aid of the legal arm to strengthen his own? Nay, verily, it is not right or manly for our man government thus to usurp the whole legal power of self-protection and defence, and leave confiding, trusting woman wholly at the mercy of this gigantic power. For perverted men will use this absolute power to abuse the defenceless, rather than protect them; and abuse of power inevitably leads to the contempt of its victim. A man who can trample on all the inalienable rights of his wife, will, by so doing, come to despise her as an inevitable consequence of wrong doing. Woman, too, is a more spiritual being than a man, and is therefore a more sensitive being, and a more patient sufferer than a man; therefore she, more than any other being, needs protection, and she should find it in that government she has sacrificed so much to uphold and sustain.

Again, I do not believe in the divorce principle. I say it is a "Secession" principle. It undermines the very vital principle of our Union, and saps the very foundation of our social and civil obligations. For example. Suppose the small, weak and comparatively feeble States in our Union were not protected by the Government in any of their State rights, while the large, strong, and powerful ones had their State rights fully guaranteed and secured to them. Would not this state of the Union endanger the rights of the defenceless ones? and endanger the Union also? Could these defenceless States resort to any other means of self-defence from the usurpation of the powerful States than that of secession? But secession is death to the Union—death to the principles of love and harmony which ought to bind the parts in one sacred whole.

Now, I claim that the Marriage Union rests on just this principle, as our laws now stand. The woman has no alternative of resort from any kind of abuse from her partner, but divorce, or secession from the Marriage Union. Now the weak States have rights as well as the strong ones, and it is the rights of the weak, which the government are especially bound to respect and defend, to prevent usurpation and its legitimate issue, secession from the Union. What we want of our government is to prevent this usurpation, by protecting us equally with our partners, so that we shall not need a divorce at all.

By equality of rights, I do not mean that woman's rights and man's rights are one and the same. By no means; we do not want the man's rights, but simply our own, natural, womanly rights. There are man's rights and woman's rights. Both different, yet both equally inalienable. There must be a head in every firm; and the head in the Marriage Firm or Union is the man, as the Bible and nature both plainly teach. We maintain that the senior partner, the man, has rights of the greatest importance, as regards the interests of the marriage firm, which should not only be respected and protected by our government, but also enforced upon them as an obligation, if the senior is not self-moved to use his rights practically—and one of these his rights, is a right to protect his own wife and children. The junior partner also has rights of equal moment to the interests of the firm, and one of these is her right to be protected by her senior partner. Not protected in a prison, but in her own home, as mistress of her own house, and as a God appointed guardian of her infant children. The government would then be protecting the marriage union, while it now practically ignores it.

To make this matter still plainer, suppose this government was under the control of the female instead of the male influence, and suppose our female government should enact laws which required the men when they entered the marriage union to alienate their right to hold their own property—their right to hold their future earnings—their right to their own homes—their right to their own offspring, if they should have any—their right to their personal liberty—and all these rights be passed over into the hands of their wives for safe keeping, and so long as they chose to be married men, all their claims on our womanly government for protection should be abrogated entirely by this marriage contract. Now, I ask, how many men would venture to get married under these laws? Would they not be tempted to ignore the marriage laws of our woman government altogether? Now, gentlemen, we are sorry to own it, this is the very condition in which your man government places us. We, women, looking from this very standpoint of sad experience, are tempted to exclaim, where is the manliness of our man government!

Divorce, I say, then, is in itself an evil—and is only employed as an evil to avoid a greater one, in many instances. Therefore, instead of being forced to choose the least of two evils, I would rather reject both evils, and choose a good thing, that of being protected in my own dear home from unmerited, unreasonable abuse—a restitution of my rights, instead of a continuance of this robbery, sanctioned by a divorce.

In short, we desire to live under such laws, as will *oblige* our husbands to treat us with decent respect, so long as our good conduct merits it, and then will they be made to feel a decent regard for us as their companions and partners, whom the laws protect from their abuse.

Second Question.

"What are your opinions, Mrs. Packard, which have caused all this rupture in your once happy family?"

My first impulse prompts me to answer, pertly, it is no one's business what I *think* but my own, since it is to God alone I am accountable for my thoughts. Whether my thoughts are right or wrong, true or false, is no one's business but my own. It is my own God given right to superintend my own thoughts, and this right I shall never guarantee to any other human being—for God himself has authorized me to "judge ye not of your own selves what is right?" Yes, I do, and shall judge for myself what is right for me to think, what is right for me to speak, and what is right for me to do—and if I do wrong, I stand amenable to the laws of society and my country; for to human tribunals I submit all my actions, as just and proper matter for criticism and control. But my thoughts, I shall never yield to any human tribunal or oligarchy, as a just and proper matter for arbitration or discipline. It is my opinion that the time has gone by for thoughts to be chained to any creeds or oligarchys; but on the contrary, these chains and restraints which have so long bound the human reason to human dictation, must be broken, for the reign of individual, spiritual freedom is about dawning upon our progressive world.

Yes, I insist upon it, that it is my own individual right to superintend my own thoughts; and I say farther, it is not my right to superintend the thoughts or conscience of any other developed being. It is none of my business what Mr. Packard, my father, or any other developed man or woman believe or think, for I do not hold myself responsible for their views. I believe they are as honest and sincere as myself in the views they cherish, although so antagonistic to my own; and I have no wish or desire to harass or disturb them, by urging my views upon their notice. Yea, further, I *prefer* to have them left entirely free and unshackled to believe just as their own developed reason dictates. And all I ask of them is, that they allow me the same privilege. My own dear father does kindly allow me this right of a developed moral agent, although we differ as essentially and materially in our views as Mr. Packard and I do. We, like two accountable moral agents, simply agree to differ, and all is peace and harmony.

My individuality has been naturally developed by a life of practical godliness, so that I now know what I do believe, as is not the case with that class in society who dare not individualize themselves. This class are mere echoes or parasites, instead of individuals. They just flow on with the tide of public sentiment, whether right or wrong; whereas the individualized ones can and do stem or resist this tide, when they think it is wrong, and in this way they meet with persecution. It is my misfortune to belong to this unfortunate class. Therefore I am not ashamed or afraid to avow my honest opinions even in the face of a frowning world. Therefore, when duty to myself or others, or the cause of truth requires it, I willingly avow my own honest convictions. On this ground, I feel not only justified, but authorized, to give the question under consideration, a plain and candid answer, knowing that this narrative of the case would be incomplete without it.

Another thing is necessary as an introduction, and that is, I do not present my views for others to adopt or endorse as their own. They are simply my individual opinions, and it is a matter of indifference to me, whether they find an echo in any other individual's heart or not. I do not arrogate to myself any popish right or power to enforce my opinions upon the notice of any human being but myself. While at the same time, I claim that I have just as good a right to my opinions as Scott, Clark, Edwards, Barnes, or Beecher, or any other human being has to theirs. And furthermore, these theologians have no more right to dictate to me what I must think and believe, than I have to dictate to them what they must think and believe. All have an equal right to their own thoughts.

And I know of no more compact form in which to give utterance to my opinions, than by inserting the following letter, I wrote from my prison, to a lady friend in Mt. Pleasant, Iowa, and sent out on my "under ground railroad." The only tidings I ever got from this letter, was a sight of it in one of the Chicago papers, following a long and minute report of my jury trial at Kankakee. I never knew how it found its way there; I only knew it was my own identical letter, since I still retain a true copy of the original among my Asylum papers. The following is a copy of the original letter, as it now stands in my own hand-writing. The friend to whom it was written has requested me to omit those portions of the letter which refer directly to herself. In compliance with her wishes, I leave a blank for such omissions. In other respects it is a true copy. The candid reader can judge for himself, whether the cherishing of such radical opinions is not a *crime* of sufficient magnitude, to justify all my wrongs and imprisonment! Is not my persecutor guiltless in this matter?

Copy of the Letter.

Jacksonville, Ill., Oct. 23d, 1861.

Mrs. Fisher. My Dear old Friend:—

My love and sympathy for you is undiminished. Changes do not sever our hearts. I cannot but respect your self-reliant, independent, and therefore progressive efforts to become more and more assimilated to Christ's glorious image. I rejoice whenever I find one who dares to rely upon their own organization, in the investigation of truth. In other words, one who dares to be an independent thinker. * * *

Yes, you, Mrs. Fisher, in your individuality, are just what God made you to be. And I respect every one who respects himself enough not to try to pervert their organization, by striving to remodel it, and thus defile God's image in them. To be natural, is our highest praise. To let God's image shine through our individuality, should be our highest aim. Alas, Mrs. Fisher, how few there are, who dare to be true to their God given nature!

That terrible dogma that our natures are depraved, has ruined its advocates, and led astray many a guileless, confiding soul. Why can we not accept of God's well done work as perfect, and instead of defiling, perverting it, let it stand in all its holy proportions, filling the place God designed it to occupy, and adorn the temple it was fitted for? I, for one, Mrs. Fisher, am determined to be a woman, true to my nature. I regard my nature as holy, and every deviation from its instinctive tendency, I regard as a perversion—a sin. To live a natural, holy life, as Christ did, I regard as my highest honor, my chief glory.

I know this sentiment conflicts with our educated belief—our Church creeds—and the honestly cherished opinions of our relatives and friends. Still I believe a "thus saith the Lord" supports it. Could Christ take upon himself our nature, and yet know no sin, if our natures are necessarily sinful? Are not God's simple, common sense teachings, authority enough for our opinions? It is, to all honest souls.

Indeed, Mrs. Fisher I have become so radical, as to call in question every opinion in my educated belief, which conflicts with the dictates of reason and common sense. I even believe that God has revealed to his creatures no practical truth, which conflicts with the common instincts of our common natures. In other words, I believe that God has adapted our natures to his teachings. Truth and nature harmonize. I believe that all truth has its source in God, and is eternal. But some perceive truth before others, because some are less perverted in their natures than others, by their educational influences, so that the light of the sun of righteousness finds less to obstruct its beams in some than in others. Thus they become lights in the world, for the benefit of others less favored. * * *

You preceded me, in bursting the shackles of preconceived opinions and creeds, and have been longer basking in the liberty wherewith Christ makes his people free, and have therefore longer been taught of him in things pertaining to life and godliness. Would that I had had the mental courage sooner to have imitated you, and thus have broken the fetters which bound me to dogmas and creeds. O, Mrs. Fisher, how trammelled and crippled our consciences have been! O, that we might have an open Bible, and an unshackled conscience! And these precious boons we shall have, for God, by his providence, is securing them to us. Yes, Mrs. Fisher, the persecutions through which we are now passing is securing to us spiritual freedom, liberty, a right, a determination to call no man master, to know no teacher but the Spirit, to follow no light or guide not sanctioned by the Word of God and our conscience—to know no "ism" or creed, but truth-ism, and no pattern but Christ.

Henceforth, I am determined to use my own reason and conscience in my investigation of truth, and in the establishment of my own opinions and practice I shall give my own reason and conscience the preference to all others. * * *

I know, also, that I am a sincere seeker after the simple truth. I know I am not willful, but conscientious, in my conduct. And, notwithstanding others deny this, I know their testimony is false. The Searcher of hearts knows that I am as honest with myself, as I am with others. And, although like Paul, I may appear foolish to others in so doing, yet my regard for truth, transcends all other considerations of minor importance. God's good work of grace in me shall never be denied by me, let others defame it, and stigmatize it as insanity, as they will. They, not I, are responsible for this sacrilegious act. God himself has made me dare to be honest and truthful, even in defiance of this heaven daring charge, and God's work will stand in spite of all opposition. "He always wins, who sides with God." Mrs. Fisher, I am not now afraid or ashamed to utter my honest opinions. The worst that my enemies can do to defame my character, they have done, and I fear them no more. I am now free to be true and honest, for this persecution for opinion and conscience' sake, has so strengthened and confirmed me in the free exercise of these inalienable rights in future, that no opposition can overcome me. For I stand by faith in what is true and right. I feel that I am born into a new element—freedom, spiritual freedom. And although the birth throes are agonizing, yet the joyous results compensate for all.

How mysterious are God's ways and plans! My persecutors verily thought they could compel me to yield these rights to human dictation, when they have only fortified them against human dictation. God saw that suffering for my opinions, was necessary to confirm me in them. And the work is done, and well done, as all God's work always is. No fear of any human oligarchy will, henceforth, terrify me, or tempt me to succumb to it.

I am not now afraid that I shall be called insane, if I avow my belief that Christ died for all mankind, and that this atonement will be effectual in saving all mankind from endless torment—that good will ultimately overcome all evil—that God's benevolent purposes concerning his creatures will never be thwarted—that no rebellious child of God's great family will ever transcend his ability to discipline into entire willing obedience to his will. Can I ever believe that God loves his children less than I do mine? * * * And has God less power to execute his kind plans than I have? Yes, I do and will rejoice to utter with a trumpet tongue, the glorious truth, that God is infinitely benevolent as well as infinitely wise and just.

Mrs. Fisher, what can have tempted us ever to doubt this glorious truth? And do we not practically deny it, when we endorse the revolting doctrine of endless punishment? I cannot but feel that the Bible, literally interpreted, teaches the doctrine of endless punishment; yet, since the teachings of nature, and God's holy character and government, seem to contradict this interpretation, I conclude we must have misinterpreted its holy teachings. For example, Jonah uses the word everlasting with a limited meaning, when he says, "thine everlasting bars are about me." Although to *his* view his punishment was everlasting, yet the issue proved that in reality, there was a limit to the time he was to be in the whale's belly. So it may be in the case of the incorrigible; they may be compelled to suffer what *to them* is endless torment, because they see no hope for them in the future. Yet the issue will prove God's love to be infinite, in rescuing them from eternal pedition.

Again, Mrs. Fisher, my determination and aim is, to become a perfect person in *Christ's* estimation, although by so doing, I may become the filth and off-scouring of all perverted humanity. What consequence is it to us to be judged of man's judgment, when the cause of our being thus condemned by them as insane, is the very character which entitles us to a rank among the archangels in heaven?

Again, I am calling in question my right to unite myself to any Church of Christ militant on earth; fearing I shall be thereby entrammelled by some yoke of bondage—that the liberty wherewith Christ makes his people free may thus be circumscribed. There is so much of the spirit of bigotry and intolerance in every denomination of Christians now on earth, that they do not allow us an open Bible and an unshackled conscience. Or, in other words, there are some to be found in almost every church, to whom we shall become stumbling blocks or rocks of offence, if we practically use the liberty which Christ offers us. Now what shall I do? I do want to obey Christ's direct command to come out from the world and be separate, while at the same time I feel that there is more Christian liberty and charity out of the Church than in it. I am now waiting and seeking the Spirit's aid in bringing this question to a practical test and issue.

And, Mrs. Fisher, I fully believe, from God's past care of me, that he will lead me to see the true and living way in which I ought to walk. I will not hide my light under a bushel, but put it upon a candlestick, that it may give light to others. I will also live out, practically, my honestly cherished opinions, believing "that they that *do* his commandments shall *know* of the doctrine." I also fully believe that the more fully and exclusively I *live out* the teachings of the Holy Spirit, the more persecution I shall experience. For they that will live godly, in Christ's estimation, "shall suffer persecution."

Mrs. Fisher, I fully believe that Christ's coming cannot be far distant. His coming will restore all things, which we have lost for his sake. Our cause will then find an eloquent pleader in Christ himself, and through our Advocate, the Judge, Himself, will acknowledge us to be his true, loyal subjects, and we shall enter into the full possession of our promised inheritance. With this glorious prospect in full view to the eye of faith, let us "gird up the loins of our mind." In other words, let us dare to pursue the course of, the *independent thinker*, and let us run with patience the race set before us. Let us carry uncomplainingly the mortifying cross, which is laid upon us, so long as God suffers it to remain; remembering that it is enough for the servant that he be as his Master. For "as they have persecuted me, they will persecute you also." "Be of good cheer." Mrs. Fisher, "I have overcome the world." Blessed consolation! Mrs. Fisher, the only response I expect to get from this letter, is your silent heartfelt sympathy in my sorrows. No utterance is allowed for my alleviation. And the only way that I am allowed to administer consolation through the pen is by stratagem. I shall employ this means so far as lies in my power, so that when the day of revelation arrives, it may be said truthfully of me, "she hath done what she could." Impossibilities are not required of us.

Please tell Theophilus, my oft repeated attempts to send him a motherly letter, have been thwarted. And he, poor persecuted boy! cannot be allowed a mother's tender, heartfelt sympathy. O, my God, protect my precious boy! and carry him safely through this pitiless storm of cruel persecution. Do be to him a mother and a sister, and God shall bless you. Please deliver this message, charged to overflowing with a mother's undying love. Be true to Jesus. Ever believe me your true friend and sympathizing sister,

E. P. W. PACKARD.

Third Question.

"Do you think, Mrs. Packard, that your husband really believes you are an insane person?"

I do not. I really believe he knows I am a sane person; and still, he is struggling with all his might to make himself and others believe this delusion, because his own conscience is accusing him constantly with this lie against it. With all his accumulated testimonials that I am insane, and all his sophistries and reasoning upon false premises to establish this lie, he cannot silence this accusing monitor within himself, testifying to the contrary. Either this is in reality the case, or he has at last reached that point, where a person has made such a sinner of his own conscience as to believe his own lies; or, in other words, he has so perverted his conscience as to become *conscientiously wrong*. But it is not for me to judge his heart, only from the standpoint of his own actions, and from this basis, I give the above as my honest opinion on this point.

Two facts alone may be sufficient to give some corroboration in support of this opinion. After taking me from my asylum prison, and while his prisoner at my own house, he asked me to sign a deed for the transfer of some of his real estate in Mt. Pleasant, Iowa, and finding I could not be induced to do it, without returning to me my note of six hundred dollars he had robbed me of, and also some of my good clothing, he sought to transfer it, as the law allows one to do, in case the needed witness is legally incapacitated by insanity to give their signature; and for this purpose he was obliged to take an *oath* that I was insane. He did take this oath that I was insane, and thereby outlawed as a legal witness. It was administered by Justice Labrie. A few days after this, he called this same Justice in to our house to witness my signing this deed, and used it as a valid signature. Now to say under oath one thing one day, and to deny it the next, is rather crooked business for a healthy Christian conscience to sanction.

Another fact. When he was preparing to put me into an Insane Asylum, I asked him why he was so very anxious to put the stigma of insanity upon me, when he knew I was not insane? Said he, "I am doing it so that your opinions need not be believed. I must protect the cause of Christ."

Cause of Christ! I felt like exclaiming, if *your* cause of Christ needs *such* a defence, I think it must be in a sad condition. If it can't stand before the opinions of a woman, I shouldn't think a man would attempt to protect it! The truth is, the cause of Christ *to him* is his creed—a set of human opinions. While the real cause of Christ is *humanity;* and a very important part of this cause of Christ to a true man, is the protection of his own wife.

Fourth Question.

"Could you forgive Mr. Packard, and live with him again as his wife?"

Yes, I could, freely, promptly and fully forgive him, on the gospel condition of *practical repentance*. This condition could secure it, and this alone. As I understand Christ's teachings, he does not allow me to forgive him until he does repent, and in some sense make restitution. He directs me to forgive my brother *if he repent*—yea, if he sins and repents seventy times seven, I must forgive as many times. But if he does not repent, I am not allowed to forgive him. And so long as he insists upon it, both by word and deed, that he has done only what was right for him to do, and that he shall do the same thing again, if he has a chance to, I do not see any chance for me to bestow my forgiveness upon a penitent transgressor.

He feels that I am the one to ask forgiveness, for not yielding my opinions to his dictation, instead of causing him so much trouble in trying to bring me under subjection to his will, in this particular. He does not claim that I ever resisted his will in any other particular—and I have not felt it my duty to do so. I had rather yield than quarrel any time, where conscience is not concerned. He knows I have done so, for twenty-one years of married life. But to tell a lie, and be false to my honest convictions, by saying I believed what I did not believe, I could not be made to do.

My truth loving nature could never be subjected to falsify itself—I must and shall be honest and truthful. And although King David said in his haste, "all *men* are liars," I rejoice he did not say all *women* were, for then there would have been no chance for my vindication of myself as a *truthful* woman! This one thing is certain, I have been imprisoned three years because I could not tell a lie, and now I think it would be bad business for me to commence at this late hour.

I cannot love oppression, wrong, or injustice under any circumstances. But on the contrary, I do hate it, while at the same time I can love the sinner who thus sins; for I find it in my heart to forgive to any extent the *penitent* transgressor. I am not conscious of feeling one particle of revengeful feeling towards Mr. Packard, while at the same time I feel the deepest kind of indignation at his abuses of me. And furthermore, I really feel that if any individual ever *deserved* penitentiary punishment, Mr. Packard does, for his treatment of me. Still, *I* would not inflict *any* punishment upon him—for this business of punishing my enemies I am perfectly content to leave entirely with my Heavenly Father, as he requires me to do, as I understand his directions. And my heart daily thanks God that it is not my business to punish him. One sinner has no right to punish another sinner. God, our Common Father, is the only being who holds this right to punish any of his great family of human children.

All that is required of me is, to do him good, and to protect myself from his abuse as best I can; and it is not doing him good to forgive him before he repents. It is reversing God's order. It is not to criminate him that I have laid the truth before the public. Duty demands it as an act of self-defence on my part, and a defence of the rights of that oppressed class of married women which my case represents. I do not ask for him to be punished at any human tribunal; all I ask is, protection for myself, and also the class I represent.

One other fact it may be well here to mention, and that is: I have withdrawn all fellowship with him in his present attitude towards me. I do not so much as speak or write to him, and this I do from the principle of self-defence, and not from a spirit of revenge. I know all my words and actions are looked upon through a very distorted medium, and whatever I say or do, he weaves into capital to carry on his persecution with. And I think I have Christ's example too as my defence in this course; for when he was convinced his persecutors questioned him only for the purpose of catching him in his words, "he was speechless." I have said all I have to say to Mr. Packard in his present character. But when he repents, I will forgive him, and restore him to full communion.

Fifth Question.

"In what estimation is Mr. Packard held in the region where these scenes were enacted?"

Where the truth is known, and as the revelations of the court room developed the facts exactly as they were found to exist, the popular verdict is decidedly against him. Indeed, the tide of popular indignation rises very high among that class, who defend religious liberty and equal rights, free thought, free speech, free press.

I state this as a fact which my own personal observation demonstrates. In canvassing for my book in many of the largest cities in the State of Illinois, I had ample opportunity to test this truth, and were I to transcribe a tithe of the expressions of this indignant feeling which I alone have heard, it would swell this pamphlet to a mammoth size. A few specimen expressions must therefore be taken as a fair representation of this popular indignation. "Mr. Packard cannot enter our State without being in danger of being lynched," is an expression I have often heard made from the common people.

From the soldiers I have often heard these, and similar expressions; "Mrs. Packard, if you need protection again, just let us know it, and we will protect you with the bullet, if there is no other defence." "If he ever gets you into another Asylum, our cannon shall open its walls for your deliverance," &c.

The Bar in Illinois may be represented by the following expressions, made to me by the Judges of the Supreme Court, in Ottawa Court house "Mrs. Packard, this is the foulest outrage we ever heard of in real life; we have read of such deep laid plots in romances, but we never knew one *acted out* in real life before. We did not suppose such a plot could be enacted under the laws of our State. But this we will say, if ever you are molested again in our State, let us know it, and we will put Mr. Packard and his conspiracy where they ought to be put."

The pulpit of Illinois almost universally condemns the outrage, as a crime against humanity and human rights. But fidelity to the truth requires me to say that there are some exceptions. The only open defenders I ever heard for Mr. Packard, came from the Church influence, and the pulpit. Among all the ministers I have conversed with on this subject, I have found only two ministers who uphold his course. One Presbyterian minister told me, he thought Mr. Packard had done right in treating me as he had; "you have no right," said he, "to cherish opinions which he does not approve, and he did right in putting you in an Asylum for it. I would treat my wife just so, if she did so!" The name and residence of this minister I could give if I chose, but I forbear to do so, lest I expose him unnecessarily.

The other clergyman was a Baptist minister. "I uphold Mr. Packard in what he has done, and I would help him in putting you in again should he attempt it." The name and place of this minister I shall withold unless self-defence requires the exposure.

When I have added one or two more church members to those two just named, it includes the whole number I ever heard defend, in my presence, Mr. Packard's course. Still, I have no doubt but that these four represent a minority in Illinois, who are governed by the same popish principles of bigotry and intolerance as Mr. Packard is. And I think it may be said of this class, as a Chicago paper did of Mr. Packard, after giving an account of the case, the writer said: "The days of bigotry and oppression are not yet past. If three-fourths of the people of the world were of the belief of Rev. Packard and his witnesses, the other fourth would be burned at the stake."

The opinion of his own church and community in Manteno, where he preached at the time I was kidnapped, is another class whose verdict the public desire to know also. I will state a few facts, and leave the public to draw their own inferences. When he put me off, his church and people were well united in him, and as a whole, the church not only sustained him in his course, but were active co-conspirators. When I returned, he preached nowhere. He was closeted at his own domicil on the Sabbath, cooking the family dinner, while his children were at church and sabbath school. His society was almost entirely broken up. I was told he preached until none would come to hear him; and his deacons gave as their reason for not sustaining him, that the trouble in his family had destroyed his influence in that community. Multitudes of his people who attended my trial, whom I know defended him at the time he kidnapped me, came to me with these voluntary confessions: "Mrs. Packard, I always knew you were not insane." "I never believed Mr. Packard's stories." "I always felt that you was an abused woman," &c., &c.

These facts indicated some change even in the opinion of his own allies during my absence. As I said, I leave the public to draw their own inferences. I have done my part to give them the premises of facts, to draw them from.

Sixth Question.

"Mrs. Packard, is your husband's real reason for treating you as he has, merely a difference in your religious belief, or is there not something back of all this? It seems unaccountable to us, that mere bigotry should so annihilate all human feeling."

This is a question I have never been able hitherto to answer, satisfactorily, either to myself or others; but now I am fully prepared to answer it with satisfaction to myself, at least; that is, facts, stubborn facts, which never before came to my knowledge until my visit home, compel me to feel that my solution of this perplexing question, is now based on the unchangeable truth of facts. For I have read with my own eyes the secret correspondence which he has kept up with my father, for about eight years past, wherein this question is answered by himself, by his own confessions, and in his own words.

And as a very natural prelude to this answer, it seems to me not inappropriate to answer one other question often put to me first, namely: "has he not some other woman in view?"

I can give my opinion now, not only with my usual promptness, but more than my usual confidence that I am correct in my opinion. I say confidently, he has *not* any other woman in view, nor never had; and it was only because I could not fathom to *the cause* of this "Great Drama," that this was ever presented to my own mind, as a question. I believe that if ever there was a man who *practically* believed in the monogomy principle of marriage, he is the man. Yes, I believe, with only one degree of faith less than that of knowledge, that the only Bible reason for a divorce never had an existence in our case.

And here, as the subject is now opened, I will take occasion to say, that as I profess to be a Bible woman both in spirit and practice, I cannot conscientiously claim a Bible right to be divorced. I never have had the first cause to doubt his fidelity to me in this respect, and he never has had the first cause to doubt my own to him.

But fidelity to the truth of God's providential events compel me to give it as my candid opinion, that the only key to the solution of this mysterious problem will yet be found to be concealed in the fact, that Mr. Packard is a *monomaniac* on the subject of woman's rights, and that it was the triumph of bigotry over his manliness, which occasioned this public manifestation of this peculiar mental phenomenon. Some of the reasons for this opinion, added to the facts of this dark drama which are already before the public, lie in the following statement.

In looking over the correspondence above referred to, I find the "confidential" part all refers to dates and occasions wherein I can distinctly recollect we had had a warm discussion on the subject of woman's rights; that is, I had taken occasion from the application of his insane dogma, namely, that "*a woman has no rights that a man is bound to respect*," to defend the opposite position of equal rights. I used sometimes to put my argument into a written form, hoping thus to secure for it a more calm and quiet consideration. I never used any other weapons in self-defence, except those paper pellets of the brain. And is not that man a coward who cannot stand before such artillery?

But not to accuse Mr. Packard of cowardice, I will say, that instead of boldly meeting me as his antagonist on the arena of argument and discussion, and there openly defending himself against my knockdown arguments, with his Cudgel of Insanity, I find he closed off such discussions with his secret "confidential" letters to my relatives and dear friends, saying, that he had sad reason to fear his wife's mind was getting out of order; she was becoming insane on the subject of woman's rights; "but be sure to keep this fact a profound secret—especially, never let Elizabeth hear that *I* ever intimated such a thing."

I presume this is not the first time an opponent in argument has called his conqueror insane, or lost to reason, simply because his logic was too sound for him to grapple with, and the will of the accuser was too obstinate to yield, when conscientiously convinced. But it certainly is more honorable and manly, to accuse him of insanity *to his face*, than it is to thus *secretly* plot against him an imprisonable offence, without giving him the least chance at self-defence.

Again, I visited Hon. Gerrit Smith, of Peterborough, New York, about three years before this secret plot culminated, to get light on this subject of woman's rights, as I had great confidence in the deductions of his noble, capacious mind; and here I found my positions were each, and all, indorsed most fully by him. Said he, " Mrs. Packard, it is high time that you *assert your rights*, there is no other way for you to live a Christian life with such a man." And, as I left, while he held my hand in his, he remarked, " You may give my love to Mr. Packard, and say to him, if he is as developed a man as I consider his wife to be a woman, I should esteem it an honor to form his acquaintance." So it appears that Mr. Smith did not consider my views on this subject as in conflict either with reason or common sense.

Again, his physician, Dr. Fordice Rice, of Cazenovia, New York, to whom I opened my whole mind on this subject, said to me in conclusion—" I can unravel the whole secret of your family trouble. Mr. Packard is a monomaniac on the treatment of woman. I don't see how you have ever lived with so unreasonable a man."

I replied, " Doctor, I can live with any man—for I will never quarrel with any one, especially a man, and much less with my husband. I can respect Mr. Packard enough, notwithstanding, to do him good all the days of my life, and no evil do I desire to do him; and moreover, I would not exchange him for any man I know of, even if I could do so, simply by turning over my hand; for I believe he is just the man God appointed from all eternity to be my husband. Therefore, I am content with my appointed portion and lot of conjugal happiness."

Again. It was only about four years before I was kidnapped, that Mr. O. S. Fowler, the great Phrenologist, examined his head, and expressed his opinion of his mental condition in nearly these words. "Mr. Packard, you are losing your mind—your faculties are all dwindling—your mind is fast running out—in a few years you will not even know your own name, unless your tread-mill habits are broken up. Your mind now is only working like an old worn out horse in a tread mill."

Thus our differences of opinion can be accounted for on scientific principles. Here we see his sluggish, conservative temperament, rejecting light, which costs any effort to obtain or use—clinging, serflike, to the old paths, as with a death grasp; while my active, radical temperament, calls for light, to bear me onward and upward, never satisfied until all available means are faithfully used to reach a more progressive state. Now comes the question. Is activity and progression in knowledge and intelligence, an indication of a sane, natural condition, or is it an unnatural, insane indication? And is a stagnant, torpid, and retrogressive state of mentality, a natural or an unnatural condition—a sane, or an insane state.?

In our mental states we simply grew apart, instead of together. He was dwindling, dying; I was living, growing, expanding. And this natural development of intellectual power in me, seemed to arouse this morbid feeling of jealousy towards me, lest I outshine him. That is, it stimulated his monomania into exercise, by determining to annihilate or crush the victim in whose mental and moral magnetism he felt so uneasy and dissatisfied with himself. While, at the same time, the influence of my animal magnetism, was never unpleasant to him; but, on the contrary, highly gratifying. Yea, I have every reason to believe he ever regarded me as a model wife, and model mother, and housekeeper. He often made this remark to me: "I never knew a woman whom I think could equal you in womanly virtues."

Again. While on this recruiting tour, I made it my home for several weeks at Mr. David Field's, who married my adopted sister, then living in Lyons, New York. I made his wife my confidant of my family trials, to a fuller degree than I ever had to any other human being, little dreaming or suspecting that she was noting my every word and act, to detect if possible, some insane manifestations. But, to her surprise, eleven weeks observation failed to develop the first indication of insanity. The reason she was thus on the alert, was, that my arrival was preceded by a letter from Mr. Packard, saying his wife was insane, and urged her to regard all my representations of family matters as insane statements. Then he added, "Now, Mrs. Field, I must require of you one thing, and that is, that you burn this letter as soon as you have read it; don't even let your husband see it at all, or know that you have had a letter from me, and by all means, keep this whole subject a profound secret from Elizabeth."

My sister, true to Mr. Packard's wishes, burned this letter, and buried the subject entirely in oblivion. But when she heard that I was incarcerated in an Asylum, then, in view of all she did know, and in view of what she did not know, she deeply suspected there was foul play in the transaction, and felt it to be her duty to tell her husband all she knew. He fully indorsed her suspicions, and they both undertook a defence for me, when she received a most insulting and abusive letter from Mr. Packard, wherein he, in the most despotic manner, tried to browbeat her into silence. Many tears did this devoted sister shed in secret over this letter and my sad fate—as this letter revealed Mr. Packard's true character to her in an unmasked state. "O, how could that dear, kind woman live with such a man!" was her constant thought.

Nerved and strengthened by her husband's advice, she determined to visit me in the Asylum, and, if possible, obtain a personal interview. She did so. She was admitted to my room. There she gave me the first tidings I ever heard of that letter. While at the Asylum, my attendants, amongst others, asked her this question: "Mrs. Field, can you tell us why such a lady as Mrs. Packard, is shut up in this Asylum; we have never seen the least exhibition of insanity in her; and one in particular said, I saw her the first day she was entered, and she was then just the same quiet, perfect lady, you see her to be to day—now do tell us why she is here?"

Her reply I will not give, since her aggravated and indignant feelings prompted her to clothe it in very strong language against Mr. Packard, indicating that he ought to be treated as a criminal, who deserved capital punishment. In my opinion, sister would have come nearer the truth, had she said he ought to be treated just as he is treating his wife—as a monomaniac.

And I hope I shall be pardoned, if I give utterance to brother's indignant feelings, in his own words, for the language, although strong, does not conflict with Christ's teachings or example. Among the pile of letters above alluded to, which Mr. Packard left accidentally in my room, was one from this Mr. Field, which seemed to be an answer to one Mr. Packard wrote him, wherein it seemed he had been calling Mr. Field to account for having heard that he had called him a "devil," and demanded of him satisfaction, if he had done so; for Mr. Field makes reply: "I do believe men are possessed with devils now a days, as much as they were in Christ's days, and I believe too that some are not only possessed with one devil, but even seven devils, and I believe *you are the man!*" I never heard of his denying the charge as due Mr. Field afterwards!

From my own observations in an insane asylum, I am fully satisfied that Mr. Field is correct in his premises, and I must also allow that he has a right of opinion in its application.

Looking from these various stand-points, it seems to me self-evident, that this Great Drama is a woman's rights struggle. From the commencement to its present stage of development, this one insane idea seems to be the backbone of the rebellion: A married woman has no rights which her husband is bound to respect.

While he simply defended his insane dogma as an *opinion* only, no one had the least right to call him a monomaniac; but when this insane idea became a *practical* one, then, and only till then, had we any right to call him an insane person. Now, if the course he has taken with me is not insanity—that is, an unreasonable course, I ask, what is insanity?

Now let this great practical truth be for one moment considered, namely, All that renders an earth-life desirable—all the inalienable rights and privileges of one developed, moral, and accountable, sensitive being, lie wholly suspended on the arbitrary will of this intolerant man, or monomaniac. No law, no friend, no logic, can defend me in the least, *legally*, from this despotic, cruel power; for the heart which controls this will has become, as it respects his treatment of me, "without understanding, a covenant breaker, without natural affection, implacable, unmerciful."

And let another truth also be borne in mind, namely, that this one man stands now as a fit representative of all that class in society, and God grant it may be found to be a very small class! who claim that the subjection of the wife, instead of the protection of the wife, is the true law of marriage. This marriage law of subjection has now culminated, so that it has become a demonstrated fact, that its track lies wholly in the direction of usurpation; and therefore this track, on which so many devoted, true women, have taken a through or life ticket upon, is one which the American government ought to guard and protect by legal enactments; so that such a drama as mine cannot be again legally tolerated under the flag of our protective government. God grant, that this one mute appeal of *stubborn fact*, may be sufficient to nerve up the woman protectors of our manly government, to guard us, in some manner, against woman's greatest foe—the women subjectors of society.

It may be proper here to add the result of this recruiting tour. After being absent eleven weeks from my home, and this being the first time I had left my husband during all my married life, longer than for one week's time, I returned to my home, to receive as cordial and as loving a welcome as any wife could desire. Indeed, it seemed to me, that the home of my husband's heart had become "empty, swept, and garnished," during my absence, and that the foul spirits of usurpation had left this citadel, as I fondly hoped, forever. Indeed, I felt that I had good reason to hope, that my logic had been calmly and impassionately digested and indorsed, during my absence, so that now this merely practical recognition of my womanly rights, almost instantly moved my forgiving heart, not only to extend to him, unasked, my full and free forgiveness for the past, but all this abuse seemed to be seeking to find its proper place in the grave of forgetful oblivion.

This radical transformation in the bearing of my husband towards me, allowing me not only the rights and privileges of a junior partner in the family firm, but also such a liberal portion of manly expressed love and sympathy, as caused my susceptible, sensitive, heart of affection fairly to leap for joy. Indeed, I could now say, what I could never say in truth before, I am happy in my husband's love—happy in simply being treated as a true woman deserves to be treated— with love and confidence. All the noblest, purest, sensibilities of woman's sympathetic nature find in this, her native element, room for full expansion and growth, by stimulating them into a natural, healthful exercise. It is one of the truths of God's providential events, that the three last years of married life were by far the happiest I ever spent with Mr. Packard.

So open and bold was I in this avowal, during these three happy years, that my correspondence of those days is radiant with this truth. And it was not three months, and perhaps not even two months, previous to my being kidnapped, that I made a verbal declaration of this fact, in Mr. Packard's presence, to Deacon Dole, his sister's husband, in these words. The interests of the Bible class had been our topic of conversation, when I had occasion to make this remark: "Brother," said I, "don't you think Mr. Packard is remarkably tolerant to me these days, in allowing me to bring my radical views before your class? And don't you think he is changing as fast as we can expect, considering his conservative organization? We cannot, of course, expect him to keep up with my radical temperament. I think we shall make a man of him yet!"

Mr. Packard laughed outright, and replied, "Well, wife, I am glad you have got so good an opinion of me. I hope I shall not disappoint your expectations!"

But, alas! where is he now? O, the dreadful demon of bigotry, was allowed to enter and take possession of this once garnished house, through the entreaties, and persuasions, and threats, of his Deacon Smith, and his perverted sister, Mrs. Dole. These two spirits united, were stronger than his own, and they overcame him, and took from him all his manly armor, so that the demon he let in, "brought with him seven other spirits more wicked than himself, and they enter in and dwell there," still; so that I sadly fear "the last state of that man will be worse than the first."

I saw and felt the danger of the vortex into which his sister and deacon were dragging him, and I tried to save him, with all the logic of love, and pure devotion to his highest and best interests; but all in vain. Never shall I forget this fatal crisis. When, just three weeks before he kidnapped me, I sat alone with him in his study, and while upon his lap, with my arms encircling his neck, and my briny cheek pressed against his own, I begged of him to be my protector, in these words: "O, husband! don't yield to their entreaties! Do be true to your marriage vow—true to yourself—true to God. Instead of taking the side of bigotry, and going against your wife, do just protect to me my right of opinion, which this deacon and sister seem determined to wrest from me. Just say to the class, "My wife has as good a right to her opinion as the class have to theirs—and I shall *protect* her in this right—you need not believe her opinions unless you choose; but she shall have her rights of opinion, unmolested, for I shall be my wife's protector." I added, "Then, husband, you will be a *man*. You will deserve honor, and you will be sure to have it; but if you become my persecutor, you will become a traitor to your manliness; you will deserve dishonor, and you will surely get it in full measure."

My earnestness he construed into anger. He thrust me from him. He determined, at all hazard, to subject my rights of opinion to his will, instead of protecting them by his manliness. The plot already laid, eight years previous, now had a rare opportunity to culminate, sure as he was of all needed help in its dreadful execution. In three short weeks I was a State's prisoner of Illinois Lunatic Asylum, being supported as a State pauper!

From this fatal evening all appeals to his reason and humanity have been worse than fruitless. They have only served to aggravate his maddened feelings, and goad him on to greater deeds of desperation. Like Nebuchadnezzar, his reason is taken from him, on this one subject; and unrestrained, maddened, resentment fills his depraved soul—his manliness is dead. Is he not a monomaniac?

FALSE REPORTS CORRECTED.

I find in circulation various false reports and misrepresentations, so slanderous in their bearing upon my character and reputation, and that of my family relatives, that I think they demand a passing notice from me, in summing up this brief record of events.

First Report.

"Mrs. Packard's mother was an insane woman, and several of her relatives have been insane; and, therefore, Mrs. Packard's insanity is hereditary, consequently, she is hopelessly insane."

This base and most cruel slander originated from Mr. Packard's own heart; was echoed before the eyes of the public, by Dr. McFarland, Superintendent of the Insane Asylum, through the Chicago Tribune, in a letter which he wrote to the Tribune in self-defence, after my trial. The verdict of the jury virtually impeached Dr. McFarland as an accomplice in this foul drama, and as one who had prostituted his high public trust, in a most notorious manner. This presentation of him and his institution before the public, seemed to provoke this letter, as a vindication of his course. And the most prominent part of this defence seemed to depend upon his making the people believe that the opinion of the jury was not correct, in pronouncing me sane. And he used this slander as the backbone of his argument, to prove that I was hopelessly insane, there having been no change either for the better or worse, while under his care, and that I left the institution just as I entered it, incurably insane.

I think I cannot answer this slander more summarily and concisely, than by quoting, verbatim, Mr. Stephen R. Moore's, my attorney, reply to this letter, as it was published at the time in the public papers.

MR. MOORE'S REPLY TO DR. MCFARLAND'S SLANDER.

"Your letter starts out with a statement of an error, which I believe to be wholly unintentional, and results from placing too much confidence in the statements of your friend, Rev. Theophilus Packard. You say, "Mrs. P., as one of the results of a strongly inherited predisposition, (her mother having been for a long period of her life insane,) had an attack of insanity previous to her marriage." Such are *not* the facts. Neither the mother, nor any blood relations of Mrs. Packard, were ever suspected or charged with being insane. And it is a slander of one of the best and most pious mothers of New England, and her ancestry, to charge her and them with insanity; and could have emanated only from the heart of the pious ———, who would incarcerate the companion of his bosom for three years, with gibbering idiots and raving maniacs.

"Nor had Mrs. Packard an attack of insanity before her marriage. The pious Packard has fabricated this story to order, from the circumstance, that when a young lady, Mrs. Packard had a severe attack of brain fever, and under which fever she was for a time delirious, and no further, has this a semblance of truth."

This is the simple truth, which all my relatives are ready, and many of them very anxious to certify to; but the limits of this pamphlet will not admit any more space in answer to this slander.

Second Report.

"Mrs. Packard is very adroit in concealing her insanity."

This report originated from the same source, and I will answer it in the words of the same writer, as found in his printed reply: "You say, 'Mrs. Packard is very adroit in concealing her insanity.' She has indeed been most adroit in this concealment, when her family physician of seven year's acquaintance, and all her friends and neighbors, with whom she visited daily, and her children, and the domestics, and lastly, the court and jury had not, and could not, discover any traces of insanity; and the only persons who say they find her insane, were Dr. McFarland, your pious friend Rev. Packard, his sister, and her husband, one deacon of the church, and a fascinating young convert—all members of his church—and a doctor. These witnesses each and every one swore upon the stand, "That it was evidence of insanity in Mrs. Packard, because she wished to leave the Presbyterian church, and join the Methodist." I quote the reasons given by these "Lambs of the Church," that you may know what weight their opinions are entitled to. The physician, upon whose certificate you say you held Mrs. Packard, swore upon the trial, that three-fourths of the religious community were just as insane as Mrs. Packard."

Third Report.

"All her family friends, almost without exception, sustain Mr. Packard in his course."

Not one of my family friends ever *intelligently* sustained Mr. Packard in his course. But they did sustain him ignorantly and undesignedly, for a time, while his tissue of lies held them back from investigating the merits of the case for themselves. But as soon as they did know, they became my firm friends and defenders, and Mr. Packard's private foes and public adversaries. I do not mean by this, that they manifest any revengeful feelings towards him, but simply a God-like resentment of his inhuman course towards me. All my relatives, without exception, who have heard my own statement from my own lips, now unite in this one opinion, that Mr. Packard has had no right nor occasion for putting me into an insane asylum.

But fidelity to the truth requires me to say in this connection, that among my family relatives, are three families of Congregational ministers—that each of these families have refused me any hearing, so that they are still in league with, and defenders of, Mr. Packard. All I have to say for them is, "May the Lord forgive them, for they know not what they do."

But it may be urged that the published certificates of her friends contradict this statement. This is not the case. Those certificates which have appeared in print since my return to my friends, all bear date to the time they were given previous to my return.

And in this connection I feel conscientiously bound, in defence of my kindred, to say, that some of these certificates are mere forgeries in its strict sense; that is, they were drafted by Mr. Packard, himself, and most adroitly urged upon the individual whose signature he desired to obtain, and thus his logic, being based in a falsehood, which was used as a truth, and received as such, they are thus made to certify to what was not the real truth. My minor children's certificates are the mere echoes of their father's will and dictation. He has tried to buy the signatures of my two oldest sons, now of age, in Chicago, by offering them some of his abundant surplus clothing, from his missionary boxes, if they would only certify that their mother was insane. But these noble sons have too much moral rectitude to sell their consciences for clothes or gold. Instead of being abettors in their father's crimes, they have, and do still, maintain a most firm stand in defence of me. And for this manly act of filial piety towards me, their father has disinherited both of them, as he has me, from our family rights.

Another thing, it is no new business for Mr. Packard to practice forgery. This assertion I can prove by his own confession. Not long before I was exiled from my home, he said to me one day, "I have just signed a note, which, if brought against me in law, would place me in a penitentiary; but I think I am safe, as I have fixed it." Again, Mr. Packard sent a great many forged letters to the Superintendent of the Asylum, while I was there, professing to come from a different source, wherein the writer urged, very strongly, the necessity of keeping me in an asylum, and begging him, most pathetically, to *keep me there*, not only for Mr. Packard's sake, but also for his children's sake, and community's sake, and, lastly, for the cause of Christ's sake! Dr. McFarland used to come to me for an explanation of this singular phenomenon. I would promptly tell him the letters are a forgery—the very face of them so speaks—for who would think of a minister in Ohio writing, self-moved, to a Superintendent in Illinois, begging of him to keep another man's wife in his Asylum! Either these letters were exact copies of Mr. Packard's, with the exception of the signature, or, they were entirely drafted from Mr. Packard's statement, and made so as to be an echo of Mr Packard's wishes, but seeming to be a self-moved act of the writer's own mind and wishes.

O, how fruitful is a depraved heart in devising lies, and masking them with the semblance of truth! and how many lies it takes to defend one! The lie he was thus trying to defend was, that I was insane, when I was not, and all this gigantic frame work of certificates and testimony became necessary as props to sustain it.

I now give the testimony of my lawyer, who, after witnessing the revelations of the court room, thus alludes to this subject in his reply to Dr. McFarland's letter. "The certificates produced, fully attesting her insanity, before she was admitted, I suspect were forgeries of the pious Packard, altered to suit the occasion, and your too generous disposition to rely upon the statements made to you, was taken advantage of again, and they were imposed upon you, without the critical examination their importance demanded."

Fourth Report.

"Mrs. Packard is alienated from her kindred, and even her own father and husband."

I will confess I am alienated from *such* manifestations of love as they showed me while in the Asylum; that is, from none at all. Not one, except my adopted sister, and my two sons at Chicago, ever made an attempt to visit me, or even wrote me scarcely one line. I do say, this was rather cold sympathy for one passing through such scenes as I was called to pass through. This fact was not only an enigma to myself, but it was so to all my Asylum friends, and even to the Doctor himself, if I can believe his own words. He would often say to me, "Mrs. Packard, who are your friends? have you any in the wide world? If so, why do they not look after you?"

I used at first to say, I have many friends, and no enemies, except Mr. Packard, that I know of in the whole world. All my relatives love me tenderly. But after watching in vain for three years of prison life for them to show me some proof of it, I changed my song, and owned up, I had no friends worth the name; for my adversity had tried or tested their love, and it had all been found wanting— entirely wanting. So it looked to me from *that* stand point. And I still insist upon it, this was a sane conclusion. For what is that love worth, that can't defend its friend in adversity? I say it is not worth the name of love.

But it must be remembered, I saw then only one side of the picture. The other side I could not see until I saw my friends, and looked from *their* standpoint. Then I found that the many letters I had written had never reached them; for Mr. Packard had instructed Dr. McFarland, and had insisted upon it, that not a single letter should be sent to any of my friends, not even my father, or sons, without reading it himself, and then sending it to him to read, before sending it; and so he must do with all the letters sent to me; and the result was, scarcely none were delivered to me, nor were mine sent to my friends. But instead of this, a brisk correspondence was kept up between Dr. McFarland and Mr. Packard, who both agreed in representing me as very insane; so much so, that my good demanded that I be kept entirely aloof from their sympathy. I have seen and read these letters, and now, instead of blaming my friends for regarding me as insane, I don't see how they could have come to any other conclusion. From *their* standpoint, they acted judiciously, and kindly.

They were anxious to aid the afflicted minister to the extent they could, in restoring reason to his poor afflicted, maniac wife, and they thought the Superintendent understood his business, and with him, and her kind husband to superintend, they considered I must be well cared for.

And again, how could they imagine, that a man would wish to have the reputation of having an insane wife, when he had not? And could the good and kind Mr. Packard neglect even his poor afflicted wife? No, she must be in good hands, under the best of care, and it is her husband on whom we must lavish our warmest, tenderest, sympathies! Yes, so it was; Mr. Packard managed so as to get all the sympathy, and his wife none at all. He got all the money, and she not a cent. He got abundant tokens of regard, and she none at all. In short, he had buried me in a living tomb, with his own hands, and he meant there should be no resurrection. And the statement that I was alienated from my friends when I was entered, is utterly *false*. No one ever loved their kindred or friends with a warmer or a purer love than I ever loved mine.

Neither was I alienated even from Mr. Packard, when he entered me. As proof of this, I will describe my feelings as indicated by my conduct, at the time he forced me from my dear ones at home. After the physicians had examined me as described in my Introduction, and Mr. Packard had ordered me to dress for a ride to the Asylum, I asked the privilege of having my room vacated, so that I might bathe myself, as usual, before dressing; intending myself to then secure about my person, *secretly*, my Bible-class documents, as all that I had said in defence of my opinions was in writing, never having trusted myself to an extemporaneous discussion of my new ideas, lest I be misrepresented. And I then felt that these documents, alone, were my only *defence*, being denied all and every form of justice, by any trial. I therefore resorted to this innocent stratagem, as it seemed to me, to secure them; that is, I did not tell Mr. Packard that I had any other reason for being left alone in my room than the one I gave him.

But he refused me this request, giving as his only reason, that he did not think it best to leave me alone. He doubtless had the same documents in view, intending thus to keep me from getting them, for he ordered Miss Rumsey to be my lady's maid, as a spy upon my actions. I dared not attempt to get them with her eye upon me, lest she take them from me, or report me to Mr. Packard, as directed by him so to do, as I believed. I resolved upon one more stratcgem as my last and only hope, and this was, to ask to be left alone long enough to pray in my own room once more, before being forced from it into my prison, When, therefore, I was all dressed, ready to be kidnapped, I asked to see my dear little ones, to bestow upon them my parting kiss. But was denied this favor also!

"Then," said I, "can I bear such trials as these without God's help? And is not this help given us in answer to our own prayers? May I not be allowed, husband, to ask this favor of God *alone* in my room, before being thus exiled from it?"

"No," said he, "I don't think it is best to let you be alone in your room."

"O, husband," said I, "you have allowed me no chance for my secret devotions this morning, can't I be allowed this one last request?"

"No; I think it is not best; but you may pray with your door open."

I then kneeled down in my room, with my bonnet and shawl on, and in the presence and hearing of the sheriff, and the conspiracy I offered up my petition, in an audible voice, wherein I laid my burdens frankly, fully, before my sympathizing Saviour, as I would have done in secret. And this Miss Rumsey reports, that the burden of this prayer was for *Mr. Packard's forgiveness.* She says, I first told God what a great crime Mr. Packard was committing in treating his wife as he was doing, and what great guilt he was thus treasuring up to himself, by this cruel and unjust treatment of the woman he had sworn before God to protect; and what an awful doom he must surely meet with, under the government of a just God, for these his great sins against me, and so forth; and then added, that if it was possible for God to allow me to bear his punishment *for him,* that he would allow me so to do, if in that way, his soul might be redeemed from the curse which must now rest upon it. In short, the burden of my prayer was, that I might be his redeemer, if my sufferings could in any possible way atone for his sins. Such a petition was, of course, looked upon by this conspiracy, as evidence of my insanity, and has been used by them, as such. But I cannot but feel that in God's sight, it was regarded as an echo of Christ's dying prayer for his murderers, prompted by the same spirit of gospel forgiveness of enemies. In fact, if I know anything of my own heart, I do know that it then cherished not a single feeling of resentment towards him.

But my soul was burdened by a sense of his great guilt, and only desired his pardon and forgiveness.

As another proof of this assertion, I will describe our parting interview at the Asylum. He had stayed two nights at the Asylum, occupying the stately guest chamber and bed alone, while I was being locked up in my narrow cell, on my narrow single bed, with the howling maniacs around for my serenaders. He sat at the sumptuous table of the Superintendent, sharing in all its costly viands and dainties, and entertained by its refined guests, for his company and companions. While I, his companion, ever accustomed to the most polished and best society, was sitting at our long table, furnished with nothing but bread and meat; and my companions, some of them, gibbering maniacs, whose presence and society must be purchased only at the risk of life or physical injury. He could walk about the city at his pleasure, or be escorted in the sumptuous carriage, while I could only circumambulate the Asylum yard, under the vigilant eye of my keeper. O, it did seem, these two days and nights, as though my affectionate heart would break with my over much sorrow. No sweet darling babe to hug to my heart's embrace—no child arms to encircle my neck and bestow on my cheek its hearty "good night" kiss. No—nothing, nothing, in my surroundings, to cheer and soothe my tempest tossed soul.

In this sorrowful state of mind Mr. Packard found me in my cell, and asked me if I should not like an interview with him, in the parlor, as he was about to leave me soon.

"Yes," said I, "I should be very glad of one," and taking his arm, I walked out of the hall. As I passed on, one of the attendants remarked: "See, she is not alienated from her husband, see how kindly she takes his arm!" When we reached the parlor, I seated myself by his side, on the sofa, and gave full vent to my long pent up emotions and feelings.

"O, husband!" said I, "how can you leave me in such a place? It seems as though I cannot bear it. And my darling babe! O, what will become of him! How can he live without his mother! And how can I live without my babe, and my children! O, do, do, I beg of you, take me home. You know I have *always* been a true and loving wife to you, and how can you treat me so?" My entreaties and prayers were accompanied with my tears, which is a very uncommon manifestation with me; and while I talked, I arose from my seat and walked the room, with my handkerchief to my eyes; for it seemed as if my heart would break. Getting no response whatever from him, I took down my hand to see why he did not speak to me when—what did I see! my husband sound asleep, nodding his head!

"O, husband!" said I, "can you sleep while your wife is in such agony?"

Said he, "I can't keep awake;.I have been broke of my rest."

"I see," said I, "there is no use in trying to move your feelings, we may as well say our 'good bye' now as ever." And as I bestowed upon him the parting kiss, I said, "May our next meeting be in the spirit land! And if there you find yourself in a sphere of lower development than myself; and you have any desire to rise to a higher plane, remember, there is one spirit in the universe, who will leave any height of enjoyment, and descend to any depth of misery, to raise you to a higher plane of happiness, if it is possible so to do. And that spirit is the spirit of your Elizabeth. Farewell! husband, forever!!"

This is the exact picture. Now see what use he makes of it. In his letter to my father, he says: "She did not like to be left. I pitied her." (Pitied her! How was his sympathy manifested?) "It was an affecting scene. But she was very mad at me, and tried to wound my feelings every way. She would send no word to the children, and would not *pleasantly* bid me good bye." Pleasantly was underlined, to make it appear, that, because I did not pleasantly bid him good bye, under these circumstances, I felt hard towards him, and this was a proof of my alienation, and is as strong a one as it is possible for him to bring in support of his charge.

Let the tender hearted mother draw her own inferences—man cannot know what I then suffered. And may a kind God grant, that no other mother may ever know what I then felt, in her own sad experience!

The truth is, I never was alienated from my husband, until he gave me just *cause* for this alienation, and not until he put me into the Asylum, and then it took four long months more, of the most intense spiritual torture, to develop in my loving, forgiving heart, one feeling of hate towards him. As proof of this, I will here insert two letters I wrote him several weeks after my incarceration.

Copy of the Letter.

Jacksonville, July 14*th,* 1860, *Sabbath, P. M.*

My Dear Children and Husband:

Your letter of July eleventh arrived yesterday. It was the third I have received from home, and, indeed, is all I have received from any source since I came to the Asylum. And the one you received from me is all I have sent from here. I thank you for writing so often. I shall be happy to answer all letters from you, if you desire it, as I see you do, by your last. I like anything to relieve the monotony of my daily routine. * * *

Dr. McFarland told me, after I had been here one week, "I do not think you will remain but a few days longer." I suspect he found me an unfit subject, upon a personal acquaintance with me. Still, unfit as I consider myself, to be numbered amongst the insane, I am so numbered at my husband's request. And for his sake, I must, until my death, carry about with me, "This thorn in the flesh—this messenger of Satan to buffet me," and probably, to keep me humble, and in my proper place. God grant it may be a sanctified affliction to me! I do try to bear it, uncomplainingly, and submissively. But, O! 'tis hard—'tis very hard. O, may you never know what it is to be numbered with the insane, within the walls of an insane asylum, not knowing as your friends will ever regard you as a fit companion or associate for them again, outside its walls.

O, the bitter, bitter cup, I have been called to drink, even to its very dregs, just because I choose to obey God rather than man! But, as my Saviour said, "the cup which my Father hath given me, shall I not drink it? O, yes, for thy sake, kind Saviour, I rejoice, that I am counted worthy to suffer the loss of all things, for thy sake. And thou hast made me worthy, by thine own free and sovereign grace. Yes, dear Jesus, I believe that I have learned the lesson thou hast thus taught me, that "in whatsoever state I am, therewith to be content."

Yes, content, to sit at a table with twenty-four maniacs, three times a day, and eat my bread and meat, and drink my milk and water, while I remember, almost each time, how many vegetables and berries are upon my own dear table at home, and I not allowed to taste, because my husband counts me unworthy, or unfit, or unsafe, to be an inmate at his fireside and table. I eat, and retire, and pray God to keep me from complaining. My fare does not agree with my health, and so I have begged of our kind attendants, to furnish me some poor, shriveled wheat, to keep in my room, to eat raw, to keep my bowels open. This morning, after asking a blessing at the table, I retired to my own room, to eat my raw, hard wheat alone, with my pine-apple to soften it, or rather to moisten it going down. Yes, the berries I toiled so very hard to get for our health and comfort, I only must be deprived of them at my husband's appointment. The past, O, the sad past! together with the present, and the unknown future. O, let oblivion cover the past—let no record of my wrongs be ever made, for posterity to see, for your sake, my own lawful husband.

O, my dear precious children! how I pity you! My heart aches for you. But I can do nothing for you. I am your father's victim, and cannot escape from my prison to help you, even you—my own flesh and blood—my heart's treasures, my jewels, my honor and rejoicing.

For I do believe you remain true to the mother who loves you so tenderly, that she would die to save you from the disgrace she has brought upon your fair names, by being stigmatised as the children of an insane mother, whom your father said he regarded as unsafe, as an inmate of your own quiet home, and, therefore, has confined me within these awful enclosures.

O, may you never know what it is to go to sleep within the hearing of such unearthly sounds, as can be heard here almost at any hour of the night! I can sleep in the hearing of it, for "so he giveth his beloved sleep." O, children dear, do not be discouraged at my sad fate, for well doing. But be assured that, although you may suffer in this world for it, you may be sure your reward will come in the next. "For, if we suffer with him, we shall also reign with him."

O, do commit your souls to him in well-doing for my sake, if you dare not for your own sake, for I do entreat you to let me be with you in heaven, if your father prevents it on earth.

I may not have much longer to suffer here on earth. Several in our ward are now sick in bed, and I give them more of my fruit than I eat myself, hoping that, when my turn comes to be sick, some one may thus serve me. But if not, I can bear it, perhaps better than they can, to be without any solace or comfort in sickness here, such as a friend needs. I have nothing to live for now, but to serve you, as I know of. But you can get along without me, can't you? Pa will take care of you. Do be kind to him, and make him as happy as possible. Yes, honor your father, if he has brought such dishonor upon your name and reputation.

I will devote my energies to these distressed objects around me, instead of attending to your wants, as a mother should be allowed to do, at least, so long as she could do so, as well as I could, and did, when I was taken from you. I know I could not, for lack of physical strength, do as much for you as I once could, still I was willing, and did do all I could for you. Indeed, I find I am almost worn out by my sufferings. I am very weak and feeble. Still, I make no complaints, for I am so much better off than many others here.

Do bring my poor lifeless body home when my spirit, which troubled your father so much, has fled to Jesus' arms for protection, and lay me by my asparagus bed, so you can visit my grave, and weep over my sad fate in this world. I do not wish to be buried in Shelburne, but let me rise where I suffered so much for Christ's sake.

O, do not, do not, be weary in well doing, for, did I not hope to meet you in heaven, it seems as though my heart would break!

I am useful here, I hope. Some of our patients say, it is a paradise here now, compared with what it was before I came. The authorities assure me, that I am doing a great work here, for the institution.

When I had the prospect of returning home in a few days, as I told you, I begged with tears not to send me, as my husband would have the same reason for sending me back as he had for bringing me here. For the will of God is still my law and guide, so I cannot do wrong, and until I become insane, I can take no other guide for my conduct. Here I can exercise my rights of conscience, without offending any one.

Yes, I am getting friends, from high and low, rich and poor. I am loved, and respected here by all that know me. I am their confident, their counsellor, their bosom friend. O, how I love this new circle of friends! There are several patients here, who are no more insane than I am; but are put here, like me, to get rid of them. But here we can work for God, and here die for him.

Love to all my children, and yourself also. I thank you for the fruit, and mirror. It came safe. I had bought one before.

I am at rest—and my mind enjoys that peace the world cannot give or take away. When I am gone to rest, rejoice for me. Weep not for me. I am, and must be forever happy in God's love.

The questions are often asked me, "Why were you sent here? you are not insane. Did you injure any one? Did you give up, and neglect your duties? Did you tear your clothes, and destroy your things? What did you do that made your friends treat such a good woman so?" Let silence be my only reply, for your sake, my husband. Now, my husband, do repent, and secure forgiveness from God, and me, before it is too late. Indeed, I pity you; my soul weeps on your account. But God is merciful, and his mercies are great above the heavens. Therefore, do not despair; by speedy repentance secure gospel peace to your tempest-tossed soul. So prays your loving wife, ELIZABETH.

EXTRACT FROM ANOTHER LETTER.

MY DEAR HUSBAND.

I thank you kindly for writing me, and thus relieving my burdened heart, by assuring me that my dear children are alive and well. I have been sadly burdened at the thought of what they are called to suffer on their mother's account. Yes, the mother's heart has wept for them every moment: yet my heart has rejoiced in God my Savior, for to suffer as well as to do His holy will, is my highest delight, my chief joy. Yes, my dear husband, I can say in all sincerity and honesty, "The will of the Lord be done." I can still by his abundant grace utter the true emotions of my full heart, in the words of my favorite verse, which you all know has been my solace in times of doubt, perplexity and trial. It is this:

> "With cheerful feet thy path of duty run,
> God nothing does, nor suffers to be done,
> But what thou wouldst thyself, couldst thou but see,
> Through all events of things as well as He."

O, the consolation the tempest tossed spirit feels in the thought that our Father is at the helm, and that no real harm can befall us with such a pilot to direct our course. And let me assure you all for your encouragement, that my own experience bears honest, practical testimony that great peace they have who make God their shield, their trust, their refuge; and I can even add that this Insane Asylum has been to me the gate to Heaven. * * *

By Dr. McFarland's leave, I have established family worship in our hall; and we never have less than twelve, and sometimes eighteen or more, quite quiet and orderly, while I read and explain a chapter—then join in singing a hymn—then kneeling down, I offer a prayer, as long as I usually do at our own family altar. I also implore the blessing of God at the table at every meal, while twenty-nine maniacs, as we are called, silently join with me. Our conversation, for the most part, is intelligent, and to me most instructive. At first, quite a spirit of discord seemed to pervade our circle. But now it is quiet and even cheerful. I find that we as individuals hold the happiness of others to a great degree in our own keeping, and that "A merry heart doeth good like medicine." * * *

If God so permit, I should rejoice to join the dear circle at home, and serve them to the best of my ability. "Nevertheless, not as I will, but as Thou wilt." I thank you, husband, for your kindness, both past and prospective. Do forgive me, wherein I have wronged you, or needlessly injured your feelings, and believe me yours,

ELIZABETH.

P. S. Tell the dear children to trust God, by doing right.

I now do frankly own, I am fully alienated from him, in his present detestable character, as developed towards me, his lawful wife. And I claim that it is not consistent with the laws of God's moral government, for a fully sane being to feel otherwise.

But it is not so with my kindred, and other friends. I am not alienated from them, for I have had no just and adequate cause for alienation. They erred ignorantly, not willfully. They were willing to know the truth; they were convicted, and are now converted to the truth. They have confessed their sin against me in thus neglecting me, and have asked my forgiveness. I have most freely forgiven them, and such penitents are fully restored to my full fellowship and confidence. To prove they are penitent, one confession will serve as a fair representation of the whole. I give it in the writer's own words, verbatim, from the letter now before me. "We are all glad you have been to visit us, and we regret we have not tried to do more for *you*, in times past. I am grieved that you have been left to suffer so much *alone*—had we known, I think something would have been done for *you*. Forgive us, won't you, for our cruel neglect?" Yes, I do rejoice to forgive them, for Christ allows me to forgive the penitent transgressor. But he does not allow me to do better than he does—to forgive the impenitent transgressor. And I do not; but as I have before said, I stand ready with my forgiveness in my heart to extend it to him, most freely, on this gospel condition of repentance—*practical* repentance.

Fifth Report.

"Dr. McFarland, the Superintendent of the Asylum, says she is insane; and he ought to *know*."

Yes, he ought to know. But, in my opinion, Dr. McFarland, does not know a sane from an insane person; or else, why does he keep so many in that Asylum, as sane as himself? And mine is not the first case a court and jury differed from him in opinion on this subject. He has been so long conversant with the insane, that he has become a perfect monomaniac on insanity and in his treatment of the insane. I never saw such inhumanity, and cruelty, and barbarity, practiced towards the innocent and helpless as he sanctions and allows in that Asylum. I could write a large volume in confirmation of this assertion, made up of scenes I myself witnessed, during my three years' incarceration in that terrible place. The matertal is all on hand for such a book, since I kept a secret journal of daily events, just as they occurred, so that my memory is not my only laboratory of such truths. And in arranging this matter for a book, I intend to turn Jacksonville Asylum inside out. That is, I shall report that Asylum from the standpoint of a patient, and if this book don't prove my assertion that Dr. McFarland is a monomaniac, I am sure it will prove him to be something worse. But I claim to defend his heart from the charge of villainy, and his intellect from imbecility, for I have often said of him, "Dr. McFarland is the *greatest* man I ever saw, and he would be the *best* if he wasn't *so bad!*"

But this is not the place to make a defence for Dr. McFarland. Let him stand where his own actions put him, for that is the only proper place for either superintendent or patient to stand upon. But I will own, God made him fit for one of his great resplendent luminaries; but Satan has marred this noble orb, so that now it has some very dark spots on its disk, such as his patients can behold without the aid of a telescope! Yes, as a general thing, his patients are not allowed to behold anything else but these dark spots, while the public are allowed to see nothing except the splendors of this luminary. And when my telescopic book is in print, the public may look, or not look, at the scenes behind the curtain, just as they please. The exact scenes are now fully daguerreotyped on my brain and heart both, as well as on my manuscript journal. In this volume I am only allowed to report what relates to myself alone. Therefore I have but little to say; for as it respects his treatment of me, individually, I regard him as a practical penitent, and on this basis, I have really forgiven him. And God only knows what a multitude of sins this man's repentance has covered! And my Christianity forbids my exposing the sins of a practical penitent, after having practically forgiven him.

As proof of his penitence, I bring this fact, that it was under his superintendence, and by his consent alone, that I was permitted to spend the last nine months of my prison life in writing "The Great Drama." This book was commenced as an act of self-defence from the charge of insanity, and this man was the first person in America that ever before allowed me any right of self-defence. And this act of practical manliness on his part, awakened, as its response, my full and hearty forgiveness of all the wrongs he had hitherto heaped upon me; and these wrongs had not been "like angels visits, few and far between." But I had, in reality, much to forgive. At least, so thought my personal friends at the Asylum, if their words echoed their real feelings. Their feelings on this subject were not unfrequently uttered in very strong language like the following: "If Mrs. Packard can forgive Dr. McFarland all the wrongs and abuses he has heaped upon her she must be more than human." And I now have before me a letter from one who had been for several years an officer in that institution, from which I will make an extract, as it corroborates this point. She says, "How the mind wanders back to those dark hours. O, that hated letter! once presented you by a ———, who delighted to torture those he could not subdue. Our hearts did pity you, Mrs. Packard. Mrs. Tenny, (now the wife of the then assistant physician, but my attendant at the time referred to,) and myself often said, everything was done that could be, to annihilate and dethrone your reason. Poor child! They had all fled—none to watch one hour! All I have to say is, if there can be found man or woman who could endure what you did in that three years, and not become a raving maniac, they should be canonized."

Yes, God, God alone, saved me from the awful vortex Mr. Packard and Dr. McFarland had prepared for me—the vortex of oblivion—God has delivered me from them who were stronger than I, and to his cause, the cause of oppressed humanity, for which I there suffered so much in its defence, I do now consecrate my spared intellect, and reason, and moral power.

This "Great Drama," written there, is my great battery, which, in God's providence, I hope sometime to get rich enough to publish;

and it is to the magnanimity of Dr. McFarland alone, under God, that my thanks are due, for letting me write this book. He dictated none o it. He allowed me perfect spiritual liberty, in penning this voluminous literary production of seven hundred pages; and if ever there was a book written wholly untrammelled by human dictation, this is the book. But as I said, his magnanimity, even at the eleventh hour, has, so far as I am concerned, secured my forgiveness.

But he has been, and I fear still is, a great sinner against others, also; for, as I have often said, it is my candid opinion, that there were fifty in that house, as patients, who have no more right to be there than the Doctor himself. Judging them from their own actions and words, there is no more evidence of insanity in them, than in Dr. McFarland's words and actions. He certainly has no scruples about keeping perfectly sane persons as patients. At first, this was to me an enigma I could not possible solve. But now I can, on the supposition that he don't know a sané from an insane person, because he has become a monomaniac on this subject, just as Mr. Packard has on the woman question. The Doctor's insane dogmas are, first: all people are insane on some points; second: insane persons have no rights that others are bound to respect.

He has never refused any one's application on the ground of their not being insane, to my knowledge, but he has admitted many whom he admitted were not near as insane as the friends who brought them were. He can see insanity in any one where it will be for his interest to see it. And let him put any one through the insane treatment he subjects his patients to, and they are almost certain to manifest some resentment, before the process is complete. And this natural resentment which his process evokes, is what he calls their insanity, or rather evidence of it. I saw the operation of his nefarious system before I had been there long, and I determined to stand proof against it, by restraining all manifestations of my resentful feelings, which his insults to me were designed to develop. And this is his grand failure in my case. He has no capital to make out his charge upon, so far as my own actions are concerned. No one ever saw me exhibit the least angry, resentful feelings. I say that to God's grace alone is this result due. I maintain, his treatment of his patients is barbarous and criminal in many cases; therefore he shows insanity in his conduct towards them.

Again, he does not always tell the truth about his patients, nor to his patients. And this is another evidence of his insanity. I do say, lying is insanity; and if I can ever be proved to be a liar, by my own words or actions, I do insist upon it I merit the charge put upon me of monomania, or insanity. But, speaking the truth, and nothing but the truth, is not lying, even if people do not believe my assertions. For the truth will stand without testimony, and in spite of all contradiction. And when one has once been proved to have lied, they have no claims on us to be believed, when they do speak the truth. Were I called to prove my assertion that the Doctor misrepresents, I could do so, by his own letters to my husband, and my father, now in my possession, and by letters Mr. Field had from him while I was in the Asylum. For example, why did he write to Mr. Field that I "was a dangerous patient, not safe to live in any private family," and then refuse to answer direct questions calling for evidence in proof on this point, and give as his reason, that he did not deem it his duty to answer impertinent questions about his patients? Simply because the assertion was a lie, and had nothing to support or defend it, in facts, as they existed. These letters abound in misrepresentations and falsehoods respecting me, and it is no wonder my friends regarded me as insane, on these representations from the Superintendent of a State Asylum.

I have every reason to think Dr. McFarland believes, in his heart, that I am entirely sane; but policy and self-interest has prompted him to deny it in words, hoping thus to destroy the influence of the sad truths I utter respecting the character of that institution. A very intelligent employee in that institution, and one who had, by her position, peculiar advantages for knowing the real state of feeling towards me in that institution, once said to me, "Mrs. Packard, I can assure you, that there is not a single individual in this house who believes you are an insane person; and as for Dr. McFarland he *knows* you are not, whatever he may choose to say upon the subject."

One thing is certain, his actions contradict his words, in this matter. Would an insane person be employed by him to carry his patients to ride, and drive the team with a whole load of crazy women, with no one to help take care of them and the team but herself? And yet Dr. McFarland employed me to do this very thing fourteen times; and I always came back safely with them, and never abused my liberty, by dropping a letter into the post-office, or any thing of the kind, and never abused the confidence reposed in me in any manner.

Would he give a crazy woman money to go to the city, and make purchases for herself? And yet he did so by me. Would a crazy woman be employed to make purchases for the house, and use as a reason for employing her, that her judgment was superior to any in the house? And yet this is true of me. Would a crazy woman be employed to cut, fit and make his wife's and daughter's best dresses, instead of a dressmaker, because she could do them better, in their opinion, than any dressmaker they could employ? And yet I was thus employed for several weeks, and for this reason. And would his wife have had her tailoress consult my judgment, before cutting her boy's clothes, and give as her reason, that she preferred my judgment and planning before her own, if I was an insane person? And yet she did.

Would the officials send their employees to me for help, in executing orders which exceeded the capacity of their own judgment to perform, if they considered my reason and judgment as impaired by insanity? And yet this was often the case. Would the remark be often made by the employees in that institution, that "Mrs. Packard was better fitted to be the matron of the institution than any one under that roof," if I had been treated and regarded as an insane person by the officials? And yet this remark was common there.

No. Dr. McFarland did not treat me as an insane person, until I had been there four months, when he suddenly changed his programme entirely, by treating me like an insane person, and ordering the employees to do so to, which order he could never enforce, except in one single instance, and this attendant soon after became a lunatic and a tenant of the poor house. My attendants said they should not treat me as they did the other patients, if the Doctor did order it.

The reason for this change in the Doctor's treatment, was not because of any change in my conduct or deportment in any respect, but because I offended him, by a reproof I gave him for his abuse of his patients, accompanied by the threat to expose him unless he repented. I gave this reproof in writing, and retained a copy myself, by hiding it behind my mirror, between it and the board-back. Several thousand copies of which are now in circulation. After this event, I was closeted among the maniacs, and did not step my foot upon the ground again, until I was discharged, two years and eight months afterwards. When he transferred me from the best ward to the worst ward, he ordered my attendants to treat me just as they did their other patients, except to not let me go out of the ward; although all the others could go to ride and walk, except myself.

Had I not known how to practice the laws of health, this close confinement would doubtless have been fatal to my good health and strong nerves. But as it was, both are still retained in full vigor.

My correspondence was henceforth put under the strictest censorship, and but few of my letters ever went farther than the Doctor's office, and most of the letters sent to me never came nearer me than his office. When I became satisfied of this, I stopped writing at all to any one, until I got an "Under Ground Express" established, through which my mail passed out, but not in.

One incident I will here mention to show how strictly and vigilantly my correspondence with the world was watched. There was a patient in my ward to be discharged ere long, to go to her home near Manteno, and she offered to take anything to my children, if I chose to send anything by her. Confident I could not get a letter out through her, without being detected, I made my daughter some under waists, and embroidered them, for a present to her from her mother. On the inside of these bleached cotton double waists, I pencilled a note to her, for her and my own solace and comfort. I then gave these into the hands of this patient, and she took them and put them into her bosom saying, "The Doctor shall never see these." But just as she was leaving the house, the Doctor asked her, if she had any letter from Mrs. Packard to her children with her? She said she had not.

He then asked her, "Have you had anything from Mrs. Packard with you?"

She said, "I have two embroidered waists, which Mrs. Packard wished me to carry to her daughter, as a present from her mother; but nothing else."

"Let me see those waists," said he.

She took them from her bosom and handed them to him. He saw the penciling. He read it, and ordered the waists to the laundry to be washed before sending them, so that no heart communications from the mother to the child, could go with them. I believe he sent them afterwards by Dr. Eddy.

In regard to Dr. McFarland's individual guilt in relation to his treatment of me, justice to myself requires me to add, that I cherish no feelings of resentment towards him, and the worst wish my heart dictates towards him is, that he may repent, and become the "Model Man" his nobly developed capacities have fitted him to become; for he is, as I have said, the greatest man I ever saw, and he would be the best if he wasn't so bad!

And the despotic treatment his patients receive under his government, is only the natural result of one of the fundamental laws of human nature, in its present undeveloped state; which is, that the history of our race for six thousand years demonstrates the fact, that absolute, unlimited power always tends towards despotism—or an usurpation and abuse of other's rights. Dr. McFarland has, in a *practical* sense, a sovereignty delegated to him, by the insane laws, almost as absolute as the marital power, which the law delegates to the husband. All of the inalienable rights of his patients are as completely subject to his single will, in the practical operation of these laws, as are the rights of a married woman to the will of her husband. And these despotic superintendents and husbands in the exercise of this power, are no more guilty, in my opinion, than that power is which licenses this deleterious element. No Republican government ought to permit an absolute monarchy to be established under its jurisdiction. And where it is found to exist, it ought to be destroyed, forthwith. And where this licensed power is known to have culminated into a despotism, which is crushing humanity, really and practically, that government is guilty in this matter, so long as it tolerates this usurpation.

Therefore, while the superintendents are guilty in abusing their power, I say that government which sustains oppression by its laws, is the first transgressor. Undoubtedly our insane asylums were originally designed and established, as humane institutions, and for a very humane and benevolent purpose; but, on their present basis, they really cover and shield many wrongs, which ought to be exposed and redressed. It is the *evils* which cluster about these institutions, and these alone, which I am intent on bringing into public view, for the purpose of having them destroyed. All the good which inheres in these institutions and officers is just as precious as if not mixed with the alloy; therefore, in destroying the alloy, great care should be used not to tarnish or destroy the fine gold with it. As my case demonstrates, they are now sometimes used for inquisitional purposes, which certainly is a great perversion of their original intent.

Sixth Report.

"Mrs. Packard's statements are incredible. And she uses such strong language in giving them expression, as demonstrates her still to be an insane woman."

I acknowledge the fact, that truth *is* stranger than fiction; and I also assert, that it is my candid opinion, that strong language is the only appropriate drapery some truths can be clothed in. For example, the only appropriate drapery to clothe a lie in, is the strong language of *lie* or *liar*, not misrepresentation, a mistake, a slip of the tongue, a deception, an unintentional error, and so forth. And for unreasonable, and inhuman, and criminal acts, the appropriate drapery is, insane acts; and an usurpation of human rights and an abuse of power over the defenceless, is appropriately clothed by the term, Despotism. And one who defends his creed or party by improper and abusive means, is a Bigot. One who is impatient and unwilling to endure, and will not hear the utterance of opinions in conflict with his own, without persecution of his opponent, is Intolerant towards him; and this is an appropriate word to use in describing such manifestations.

And here I will add, I do not write books merely to tickle the fancy, and lull the guilty conscience into a treacherous sleep, whose waking is death. Nor do I write to secure notoriety or popularity. But I do write to defend the cause of human rights; and these rights can never be vindicated, without these usurpations be exposed to public view, so that an appeal can be made to the public conscience, on the firm basis of unchangeable truth—the truth of facts as they do actually exist. I know there is a class, but I fondly hope they are the minority, who will resist this solid basis even—who would not believe the truth should Christ himself be its medium of utterance and defence. But shall I on this account withold the truth, lest such cavilers reject it, and trample it under foot, and then turn and rend me with the stigma of insanity, because I told them the simple truth? By no means. For truth is not insanity; and though it may for a time be crushed to the earth, it shall rise again with renovated strength and power. Neither is strong and appropriate language insanity. But on the contrary, I maintain that strong language is the only suitable and appropriate drapery for a reformer to clothe his thoughts in, notwithstanding the very unsuitable and inappropriate stigma of Insanity which has always been the reformer's lot to bear for so doing in all past ages, as well as the present age.

Even Christ himself bore this badge of a Reformer, simply because he uttered truths which conflicted with the established religion of the church of his day. And shall I repine because I am called insane for the same reason? It was the spirit of bigotry which led the intolerant Jews to stigmatize Christ as a madman, because he expressed opinions differing from their own. And it is this same spirit of bigotry which has been thus intolerant towards me. And it is my opinion that bigotry is the most implacable, unreasonable, unmerciful feeling that can possess the human soul. And it is my fervent prayer that the eyes of this government may be opened to see, that the laws do not now protect or shield any married woman from this same extreme manifestation of it, such as it has been my sad lot to endure, as the result of this legalized persecution.

NOTE OF THANKS TO MY PATRONS.

I deem it appropriate in this connection, to express the gratitude I feel for the kind, practical sympathy, and liberal patronage, which has been extended to me by the public, through the sale of my books. Had it not been for your generous patronage, my kind patrons, I, and the noble cause I represent, would have been crushed to the earth, so far as my influence was concerned. For with no law to shield me, and with no "greenbacks" to defend myself with, what could I have done to escape another imprisonment, either in some asylum or poorhouse?

It has been, and still is, the verdict of public sentiment, which the circulation of these books has developed, that has hitherto shielded me from a second kidnapping. And this protection you have kindly secured to me by buying my books. I would willingly have given my books a gratuitous circulation to obtain this protection, if I could possibly have done so. But where could the $3000.00 I have paid out for the expense of printing and circulating these books have been obtained? No one could advance me money safely, so long as I was Mr. Packard's lawful wife, and I could not even get a divorce, without the means for prosecuting the suit. Indeed, it was your patronage alone, which could effectually help me on to a self-reliant platform—the platform of "greenback independence."

I have never made any appeal to the charities of the public, neither can I do so, from principle. For so long as I retain as good health as it is my blessed privilege still to enjoy, I feel conscientiously bound to work for my living, instead of living on the toil of others. My strong and vigorous health is the only capital that I can call my own. All my other natural, inalienable rights, are entirely in the hands of my persecutor, and subject to his control. But while this capital holds good, I am not a suitable object of charity. I am prosecuting business on business principles, and I am subject to the same laws of success or failure as other business persons are. I intend, and hope to make my business lucrative and profitable, as well as philanthropic and benevolent.

I maintain that I have no claims upon the charities of the public, while at the same time I maintain that I have a claim upon the sympathies of our government. It is our government, the man government of America, who have placed me in my deplorable condition; for I am just where their own laws place me, and render all other married women *liable* to be placed in the same position. It is the "Common Law" which our government took from English laws which makes a nonentity of a married woman, whose existence is wholly subject to another, and whose identity is only recognized through another. In short, the wife is dead, while her husband lives, as to any legal existence. And where the Common Law is not modified, or set aside by the Statute Laws, this worst form of English despotism is copied as a model law for our American people!

Yes, I feel that I have a just claim upon the sympathies of our government. Therefore, in selling my books, I have almost entirely confined my application to the men, not the women, for the men alone constitute the American government. And my patrons have responded to my claims upon their sympathy, in a most generous, and praiseworthy manner. Yea, so almost universally have I met with the sympathy of those gentlemen that I have freely conversed with on this subject, that I cherish the firm conviction, that our whole enlightened government would "en masse," espouse the principles I defend, and grant all, and even more than I ask for married woman, could they but see the subject in the light those now do, whom I have conversed with on this subject. I am fully satisfied that all that our manly government needs to induce them to change this "Common Law" in relation to woman is, only to know what this law is, and how cruelly it subjects the women in its practical application. For man is made, and constituted by God himself, to be the protector of woman. And when he is true to this his God given nature, he is her protector. And all true men who have not perverted or depraved their God-like natures, will, and do, as instinctively protect their own wives, as they do themselves. And the wives of such men do not need any other law, than this law of manliness, to protect them or their interests.

But taking the human race as they now are, we find some exceptions to this general rule. And it is for these exceptions that the law is needed, and not for the great masses. Just as the laws against crimes are made for the criminals, not for the masses of society, for they do not need them; they are a law unto themselves, having their own consciences for their Judges and Jurors. I see no candid, just reason why usurpation, and injustice, and oppression, should not be legislated against, in this form, as well as any other. Developed, refined, sensitive woman, is as capable of feeling wrongs as any other human being. And why should she not be legally protected from them as well as a man? My confidence in this God-like principle of manliness is almost unbounded. Therefore I feel that a hint is all that is needed, to arouse this latent principle of our government into prompt and efficient action, that of extending legal protection to subjected married woman.

There is one word I will here say to my patrons, who have the first installment of my "Great Drama" in their possession, that you have doubtless found many things in that book which you cannot now understand, and are therefore liable to misinterpret and misapprehend my real meaning. I therefore beg of you not to judge me harshly at present, but please suspend your judgment until this allegory is published entire, and then you will be better prepared to pass judgment upon it. Supposing Bunyan's allegory of his Christian pilgrim had isolated parts of it published, separate from the whole, and we knew nothing about the rest, should we not be liable to misinterpret his real meaning?

Another thing, I ask you to bear in mind, this book was written when my mind was at its culminating point of spiritual or mental torture, as it were, and this may serve in your mind as an excuse, for what may seem to you, as extravagant expressions; while to me, they were only the simple truth as I experienced it. No one can judge of these feelings correctly, until they have been in my exact place and position; and since this is an impossibility, you have a noble opportunity for the exercise of that charity towards me which you would like to have extended to yourselves in exchange of situations.

A person under extreme physical torture, gives utterance to strong expressions, indicating extreme anguish. Have we, on this account, any reason or right to call him insane? So a person in extreme spiritual or mental agony, has a right to express his feelings in language corresponding to his condition, and we have no right to call him insane for doing so.

Upon a calm and candid review of these scenes, from my present standpoint, I do maintain that the indignant feelings which I still cherish towards Mr. Packard, and did cherish towards Dr. McFarland, for their treatment of me, were not only natural, sane feelings, but also were Christian feelings. For Christ taught us, both by his teachings and example, that we ought to be angry at sin, and even hate it, with as marked a feeling as we loved good. "I, the Lord, hate evil." And so should we. But at the same time we should not sin, by carrying this feeling so far, as to desire to revenge the wrong-doer, or punish him ourselves, for then we go too far to exercise the feeling of forgiveness towards him, even if he should repent. We are not then following Christ's directions, "Be ye angry and sin not." Now I am not conscious of ever cherishing one revengeful feeling towards my persecutors; while, at the same time, I have prayed to God, most fervently, that he would inflict a just punishment upon them for their sins against me, if they could not be brought to repent without. For my heart has ever yearned to forgive them, from the first to the last, on this gospel condition.

I think our government has been called to exercise the same kind of indignation towards those conspirators who have done all they can do to overthrow it; and yet, they stand ready to forgive them, and restore them to their confidence, on the condition of practical repentance. And I say further, that it would have been wrong and sinful for our government to have witheld this expression of their resentment towards them, and let them crush it out of existence, without trying to defend itself. I say it did right in defending itself with a resistance corresponding to the attack. So I, in trying to defend myself against this conspiracy against my personal liberty, have only acted on the self-defensive principle. Neither have I ever aggressed on the rights of others in my self-defence. I have simply defended my own rights.

In my opinion, it would be no more unreasonable to accuse the inmates of "Libby Prison" with insanity, because they expressed their resentment of the wrongs they were enduring in strong language, than it is to accuse me of insanity for doing the same thing while in my prison. For prison life is terrible under any circumstances. But to be confined amongst raving maniacs, for years in succession, is horrible in the extreme. For myself, I should not hesitate one moment which to choose, between a confinement in an insane asylum, as I was, or being burned at the stake. Death, under the most aggravated forms of torture, would now be instantly chosen by me, rather than life in an insane asylum. And whoever is disposed to call this "strong language," I say, let them try it for themselves as I did, and *then* let them say whether the expression is any stronger than the case justifies. For until they have tried it, they can never imagine the horrors of the maniac's ward in Jacksonville Insane Asylum.

In this connection it may be gratifying to my patrons and readers both, to tell them how I came to write *such* a book, instead of an ordinary book in the common style of language. It was because such a kind of book was presented to my mind, and no other was. It was under these circumstances that this kind of inspiration came upon me.

The day after my interview with the Trustees, the Doctor came to my room to see what was to be done. His first salutation was, "Well, Mrs. Packard, the Trustees seemed to think that you hit your mark with your gun."

"Did they?" said I. "And was it that, which caused such roars and roars of laughter from the Trustees' room after I left?"

"Yes. Your document amused them highly. Now, Mrs. Packard, I want you to give me a copy of that document, for what is worth hearing once is worth hearing twice."

"Very well," said I, "I will. And I should like to give the Trustees a copy, and send my father one, and some others of the Calvinistic clergy. But it is so tedious for me to copy anything, how would it do to get a few handbills or tracts printed, and send them where we please?"

"You may," was his reply, "and I will pay the printer."

"Shall I add anything to it; that is, what I said to the Trustees, and so forth?"

"Yes, tell the whole! Write what you please!"

With this most unexpected license of unrestricted liberty, I commenced re-writing and preparing a tract for the press. But before twenty-four hours had elapsed since this liberty license was granted to my hitherto prison-bound intellect, the vision of a big book began to dawn upon my mind, accompanied with the most delightful feelings of satisfaction with my undertaking. And the next time the Doctor called, I told him, that it seemed to me that I must write a book—a *big book*—and "that is the worst of it," said I, "I don't want a large book, but I don't see how I can cut it down, and do it justice. I want to lay two train of cars," said I, "across this continent—the Christian and the Calvinistic. Then I want to sort out all the good and evil found in our family institutions, our Church and State institutions, and our laws, and all other departments of trades and professions, &c., and then come on with my two train of cars, and gather up this scattered freight, putting the evil into the Calvinistic train, and the good into the Christian train, and then engineer them both on to their respective terminus. These thoughts are all new and original with me, having never thought of such a thing, until this sort of mental vision came before my mind. What shall I do, Doctor?"

"Write it out just as you see it."

He then furnished me with paper and gave directions to the attendants to let no one disturb me, and let me do just as I pleased. And I commenced writing out this mental vision; and in six week's time I penciled the substance of "The Great Drama," which, when written out for the press, covers two thousand five hundred pages! Can I not truly say my train of thought was engineered by the "Lightning Express?" This was the kind of inspiration under which my book was thought out and written. I had no books to aid me, but Webster's large Dictionary and the Bible. It came wholly through my own reason and intellect, quickened into unusual activity by some spiritual influence, as it seemed to me. The production is a remarkable one, as well as the inditing of it a very singular phenomenon.

The estimation in which the book is held by that class in that Asylum who are "spirit mediums," and whose only knowledge of its contents they wholly derive from their clairvoyant powers of reading it, without the aid of their natural vision, it may amuse a class of my readers to know. It was a fact the attendants told me of, that my book and its contents, was made a very common topic of remark in almost every ward in the house; while all this time, I was closeted alone in my room writing it, and they never saw me or my book. I would often be greatly amused by the remarks they made about it, as they were reported to me by witnesses who heard them. Such as these: "I have read Mrs. Packard's book through, and it is the most amusing thing I ever read." "Calvinism is dead—dead as a herring." "Mrs. Packard drives her own team, and she drives it beautifully, too." "The Packard books are all over the world, Norway is full of them. They perfectly devour the Packard books in Norway." "Mrs. Packard finds a great deal of fault with the Laws and the Government, and she has reason to." "She defends a higher and better law than our government has, and she'll be in Congress one of these days, helping to make new laws!"

If this prophetess had said that *woman's influence* would be felt in Congress, giving character to the laws, I might have said I believed she had uttered a true prophecy.

One very intelligent patient, who was a companion of mine, and had read portions of my book, came to my room one morning with some verses which she had penciled the night previous, by moonlight, on the fly-leaf of her Bible, which she requested me to read, and judge if they were not appropriate to the character of my book. She said she had been so impressed with the thought that she must get up and write something, that she could not compose herself to sleep until she had done so; when she wrote these verses, but could not tell a word she had written the next morning, except the first line. I here give her opinions of the book in her own poetic language, as she presented them to me.

LINES SUGGESTED BY THE PERUSAL OF THE GREAT DRAMA.

Affectionately presented to the "World's Friend"—Mrs. E. P. W. Packard—by her friend, Mrs. Sophia N. B. Olsen.

Go, little book, go seek the world;
With banner new, with flag unfurled;
Go, teach mankind aspirings high,
By *human* immortality!

Thou canst not blush; thine open page
Will all our higher powers engage;
Thy name on every soul shall be,
Defender of humanity!

8

The poor, the sad, the sorrowing heart,
Shall joy to see thy book impart
Solace, to every tear-dimmed eye,
That's wept, till all its tears are dry.

The palid sufferer on the bed
Of sickness, shall erect the head
And cry, "Life yet hath charms for me
When Packard's books shall scattered be."

Each prison victim of despair
Shall, in thy book, see written there
Another gospel to thy race,
Of sweet "Requiescat in pace."

The time-worn wigs, with error gray,
Their dusty locks with pale dismay,
Shall shake in vain in wild despair,
To see their prostrate castles, where?

No mourner's tear shall weep their doom,
No bard shall linger o'er their tomb,
No poet sing, but howl a strain
Farewell, thou doom'd, live not again.

Yes, oh, poor Ichabod must lay,
Deep buried in Aceldema!
His lost Consuelo shall rise
No more, to cheer his death-sealed eyes.

Then speed thy book, oh, sister, speed,
The waiting world thy works must read;
Bless'd be the man who cries, "Go on,"
"Hinder it not, it shall be gone."

Go, little book, thy destiny
Excelsior shall ever be;
A fadeless wreath shall crown thy brow,
O writer of that book! e'en now.

The wise shall laugh—the foolish cry—
Both wise and foolish virgins, why?
Because the first will wiser grow,
The foolish ones some wisdom show.

<pre>
The midnight cry is coming soon,
The midnight lamp will shine at noon;
I fear for some, who snoring lie,
Then rise, ye dead, to judgment fly.

The stars shall fade away—the sun
Himself grow dim with age when done
Shining upon our frigid earth;
But Packard's book shall yet have birth,
But never death, on this our earth.
</pre>

JACKSONVILLE LUNATIC ASYLUM, Jan. 27, 1863.

So much for the opinions of those whom this age call crazy, but who are, in my opinion, no more insane than all that numerous class of our day, who are called "spirit mediums;" and to imprison them as insane, simply because they possess these spiritual gifts or powers, is a barbarity, which coming generations will look upon with the same class of emotions, as we now look upon the barbarities attending Salem Witchcraft. It is not only barbarous and cruel to deprive them of their personal liberty, but it is also a crime against humanity, for which our government must be held responsible at God's bar of justice.

I will now give some of the opinions of a few who know something of the character of my book, whom the world recognize as sane. Dr. McFarland used to sometimes say, "Who knows but you were sent here to write an allegory for the present age, as Bunyan was sent to Bedford Jail to write his allegory?" Dr. Tenny, the assistant physician, once said to me as he was pocketing a piece of my waste manuscript, "I think your book may yet become so popular, and acquire so great notoriety, that it will be considered an honor to have a bit of the paper on which it was written!"

I replied, "Dr. Tenny, you must not flatter me."

Said he, "I am not flattering, I am only uttering my honest opinions."

Said another honorable gentleman who thought he understood the character of the book, "Mrs. Packard, I believe your book will yet be read in our Legislative Halls and in Congress, as a specimen of the highest form of law ever sent to our world, and coming millions will read your history, and bless you as one who was afflicted for humanity's sake." It must be acknowledged that this intelligent gentleman had some solid basis on which he could defend this extravagant opinion, namely: that God does sometimes employ "the weak things of the world to confound the mighty."

These expressions must all be received as mere human opinions, and nothing more. The book must stand just where its own intrinsic merits place it. If it is ever published, it, like all other mere human productions, will find its own proper level, and no opinions can change its real intrinsic character. The great question with me is, how can I soonest earn the $2,500.00 necessary to print it with? Should I ever be so fortunate as to gain that amount by the sale of this pamphlet, I should feel that my great life-work was done, so that I might feel at full liberty to rest from my labors. But until then, I cheerfully labor and toil to accomplish it.

NOTE OF THANKS TO THE PRESS.

In this connection, I deem it right and proper that I should acknowledge the aid I have received from the public Press—those newspapers whose manliness has prompted them to espouse the cause of woman, by using their columns to help me on in my arduour enterprise. My object can only be achieved, by enlightening the public mind into the need and necessities of the case. The people do not make laws until they see the need of them. Now, when one case is presented showing the need of a law to meet it, and this is found to be a representative case, that is, a case fairly representing an important class, then, and only till then, is the public mind prepared to act efficiently in reference to it. And as the Press is the People's great engine of power in getting up an agitation on any subject of public interest, it is always a great and desirable object to secure its patronage in helping it forward. This help it has been my good fortune to secure, both in Illinois and Massachusetts.

And my most grateful acknowledgments are especially due the Journal of Commerce of Chicago, also the Chicago Tribune, the Chicago Times, the Post, the New Covenant, and the North Western Christian Advocate. All these Chicago Journals aided me more or less in getting up an agitation in Illinois, besides a multitude of other papers throughout that State too numerous to mention.

Some of the papers in Massachusetts, to whom my acknowledgments are due, are the Boston Journal, the Transcript, the Traveller, the Daily Advertiser, the Courier, the Post the Recorder, the Commonwealth, the Investigator, the Nation, the Universalist, the Christian Register, the Congregationalist, the Banner of Light, and the Liberator. All these Boston Journals have aided me, more or less, in getting up an excitement in Massachusetts, and bringing the subject before the Massachusett's Legislature. Many other papers throughout the State have noticed my cause with grateful interest.

As the public come to apprehend the merits of my case, and look upon it as a mirror, wherein the laws in relation to married women are reflected, they will doubtless join with me in thanks to these Journals who have been used as means of bringing this light before them.

TESTIMONIALS.

Although my cause, being based in eternal truth, does not depend upon certificates and testimonials to sustain it, and stands therefore in no need of them; yet, as they are sometimes called for, as a confirmation of my statements, I have asked for just such testimonials as the following gentlemen felt self-moved to give me. I needed no testimonials while prosecuting my business in Illinois, for the facts of the case were so well known there, by the papers reporting my trial so generally. I needed no other passport to the confidence of the public.

But when I came to Boston to commence my business in Massachusetts, being an entire stranger there, I found the need of some credentials or testimonials in confirmation of my strange and novel statements. And it was right and proper, under such circumstances, that I should have them. I therefore wrote to Judge Boardman and Hon. S. S. Jones, my personal friends, in Illinois, and told them the difficulty I found in getting my story believed, and asked them to send me anything in the form of a certificate, that they in their judgment felt disposed to send me, that might help me in surmounting this obstacle. Very promptly did these gentlemen respond to my request, and sent me the following testimonials, which were soon printed in several of the Boston papers, with such editorials accompanying them, as gave them additional weight and influence in securing to me the confidence of the public.

Judge Boardman is an old and distinguished Judge in Illinois, receiving, as he justly merits, the highest esteem and confidence of his cotemporaries, as a distinguished scholar, an eminent Judge, and a practical Christian.

Mr. Jones is a middle aged man, of the same stamp as the Judge, receiving proof of the esteem in which he is held by his cotemporaries, in being sent to Congress by vote of Illinois' citizens, and by having been for successive years a member of the Legislature of that State. He was in that position when he sent me his certificate.

JUDGE BOARDMAN'S LETTER.

To all persons who would desire to give sympathy and encouragement to a most worthy but persecuted woman!

The undersigned, formerly from the State of Vermont, now an old resident of the State of Illinois, would most respectfully and fraternally certify and represent: That he has been, formerly and for many years, associated with the legal profession in Illinois, and is well known in the north-eastern part of said State. That in the duties of his profession and in the offices he has filled, he has frequently investigated, judicially, and otherwise, cases of insanity. That he has given considerable attention to medical jurisprudence, and studied some of the best authors on the subject of insanity; has paid great attention to the principles and philosophy of mind, and therefore would say, with all due modesty, that he verily believes himself qualified to give an opinion entitled to respectful consideration, on the question of the sanity or insanity of any person with whom he may be acquainted. That he is acquainted with Mrs. E. P. W. Packard, and verily believes her not only sane, but that she is a person of very superior endowments of mind and understanding, naturally possessing an exceedingly well balanced organization, which, no doubt, prevented her from becoming insane, under the persecution, incarceration, and treatment she has received. That Mrs. Packard has been the victim of *religious bigotry*, purely so, without a single circumstance to alleviate the darkness of the transaction! A case worthy of the palmiest days of the inquisition!!

The question may be asked, how this could happen, especially in Northern Illinois? To which I answer that the common law prevails here, the same as in other States, where this law has not been modified or set aside by the statute laws, which gives the legal custody of the wife's person, into the hands of the husband, and therefore, a wife can only be released from oppression, or even from imprisonment by her husband, by the legal complaint of herself, or some one in her behalf, before the proper judicial authorities, and a hearing and decision in the case; as was finally had in Mrs. Packard's case, she having been in the first place, taken by force, by her husband, and sent to the Insane Hospital, without any opportunity to make complaint, or without any hearing or investigation.

But how could the Superintendent of the Insane Hospital be a party to so great a wrong? Very easily answered, without necessarily impeaching his honesty, when we consider that her alleged insanity was on religious subjects; her husband a minister of good standing in his denomination, and the Superintendent sympathizing with him, in all probability, in religious doctrine and belief, supposed, of course, that she was insane. She was legally sent to him, by the authority of her husband, as insane; and Mrs. Packard had taught doctrines similar to the Unitarians and Universalists and many radical preachers; and which directly opposed the doctrine her husband taught, and the doctrine of the Church to which he and Mrs. Packard belonged; the argument was, that of course the woman must be crazy!! And as she persisted in her liberal sentiments, the Superintendent persisted in considering that she was insane! However, whether moral blame should attach to the Superintendent and Trustees of the Insane Hospital, or not, in this transaction, other than prejudice, and learned ignorance; it may now be seen, from recent public inquiries and suggestions, that it is quite certain, that the laws, perhaps in all the States in relation to the insane, and their confinement and treatment, have been much abused, by the artful and cunning, who have incarcerated their relatives for the purpose of getting hold of their property; or for difference of opinion as to our state and condition in the future state of existence, or religious belief.

The undersigned would further state: That the published account of Mrs. Packard's trial on the question of her sanity, is no doubt perfectly reliable and correct. That the Judge before whom she was tried, is a man of learning, and ability, and high standing in the judicial circuit, in which he presides. That Mrs. Packard is a person of strict integrity and truthfulness, whose character is above reproach. That a history of her case after the trial, was published in the daily papers in Chicago, and in the newspapers generally, in the State; arousing at the time, a public feeling of indignation against the author of her persecution, and sympathy for her; that nothing has transpired since, to overthrow or set aside the verdict of popular opinion; that it is highly probable that the proceedings in this case, so far as the officers of the State Hospital for the insane are concerned, will undergo a rigid investigation by the Legislature of the State.

The undersigned understands that Mrs. Packard does not ask pecuniary charity, but that sympathy and paternal assistance which may aid her to obtain and make her own living, she having been left by her husband, without any means, or property whatever.

All of which is most fraternally and confidently submitted to your kind consideration. WILLIAM A. BOARDMAN.
WAUKEGAN, ILL., DEC. 3, 1864.

HON. S. S. JONES' LETTER.

"*To a kind and sympathizing public :—*

This is to certify that I am personally acquainted with Mrs. E. P. W. Packard, late an inmate of the Insane Asylum of the State of Illinois. That Mrs. Packard was a victim of a foul and cruel conspiracy I have not a single doubt, and that she is and ever has been as sane as any other person, I verily believe. But I do not feel called upon to assign reasons for my opinion, in the premises, as her case was fully investigated before an eminent Judge of our State, and after a full and careful examination, she was pronounced sane, and restored to liberty.

Still I repeat, but for the cruel conspiracy against her, she could not have been incarcerated, as a lunatic, in an asylum. Whoever reads her full and fair report of her case, will be convinced of the terrible conspiracy that was practiced towards a truly thoughtful and accomplished lady. A conspiracy worthy of a demoniac spirit of ages long since passed, and such as we should be loth to believe could be practiced in this enlightened age, did not the records of our court verify its truth.

To a kind and sympathizing public I commend her. The deep and cruel anguish she has had to suffer, at the hands of those who should have been her protectors, will, I doubt not, endear her to you, and you will extend to her your kindest sympathy and protection.

Trusting through her much suffering the public will become more enlightened, and that our noble and benevolent institutions—the asylums for the insane—will never become perverted into institutions of cruelty and oppression, and that Mrs. Packard may be the last subject of such a conspiracy as is revealed in her books, that w ..l ever transpire in this our State of Illinois, or elsewhere.

Very respectfully,   S. S. JONES."

ST. CHARLES, ILL., DEC. 2, 1864.

EDITORIAL REMARKS.

"Assuming, as in view of all the facts it is our duty to do, the correctness of the statements made by Mrs. Packard, two matters of vital importance demand consideration:

1. What have 'the rulers in the church' done about the persecution? They have not publicly denied the statements; virtually (on the principle that under such extraordinary circumstances silence gives consent,) they concede their correctness. Is the wrong covered up? the guilty party allowed to go unchallenged lest "the cause" suffer by exposure?" If they will explain the matter in a way to exculpate the accused, these columns shall be prompt to do the injured full and impartial justice. We are anxious to know what they have to say in the premises. If Mrs. Packard *is* insane because she rejects Calvinism, then *we* are insane, liable to arrest, and to be placed in an insane asylum! We have a *personal* interest in this matter.

2. Read carefully Judge Boardman's statement as to the bearing of "common law" on Mrs. Packard's case. If a bad man, hating his wife and wishing to get rid of her, is base enough to fabricate a charge of insanity, and can find two physicians "in regular standing" foolish or wicked enough to give the legal certificate, the wife is helpless! The "common law" places her wholly at the mercy of her brutal lord. Certainly the statute should interfere. Humanity, not to say Christianity, demands, that special enactments shall make impossible, such atrocities as are alleged in the case of Mrs. Packard— atrocities which, according to Judge Boardman, *can* be enacted in the name of "common law." We trust the case now presented will have at least the effect, to incite Legislative bodies to such enactments as will protect women from the possibility of outrages, which, we are led to fear, ecclesiastical bodies had rather cover up, than expose and rebuke to the prejudice of sectarian ends—the 'sacred cause.'"

As I have said, there was a successful effort made in the Massachusett's Legislature to change the laws in reference to the mode of commitment into Insane Asylums that winter, 1865, and as Hon. S. E. Sewall was my "friend and fellow laborer," as he styles himself, in that movement, I made application to him this next winter, for such a recommend as I might use to aid me in bringing this subject before the Illinois' Legislature this winter, for the purpose of getting a change in their laws also. But finding that the Illinois' Legislature do not meet this year, I have had no occasion to use it, as I intended. Having it thus on hand, I will add this to the foregoing.

HON. S. E. SEWALL'S TESTIMONIAL.

"I have been acquainted with Mrs. E. P. W. Packard for about a year, I believe. She is a person of great religious feeling, high moral principle, and warm philanthropy. She is a logical thinker, a persuasive speaker, and such an agitator, that she sometimes succeeds where a man would fail. I think she will be very useful in the cause to which she has devoted herself, I mean procuring new laws to protect married women.

I give Mrs. Packard these lines of recommendation, because she has asked for them. I do not think them at all necessary, for she can recommend herself, far better than I can. S. E. SEWALL."

BOSTON, Nov. 27, 1865.

After these testimonials, and the editorial remarks accompanying them had appeared in these Boston journals, Mr. Packard sent various articles to these journals in reply, designing to counteract their legitimate influence in defence of my course. Some of these articles were published, and many were refused, by the editors. The "Universalist," and the "Daily Advertiser," published a part of his voluminous defence, which was made up almost entirely of certificates and credentials, but no denial of the truth of the general statement. The chief point in his defence which he seemed the most anxious to establish was, that my trial was not correctly reported—and not a fair trial—a mere mob triumph, instead of a triumph of justice. One of these papers, containing his impeachments of the court, was sent to Kankakee City, Illinois, where the court was held, and elicited many prompt and indignant replies. An article soon appeared in the Kankakee paper, on this subject, stating his defamations against the judge, lawyers, and jury, and then added, "Mr. Packard is both writing his wife into notoriety, and himself into infamy," by his publishing such statements, as he would not dare to publish in Illinois;

and it was astonishing to them, how such a paper as the Boston "Daily Advertiser," should allow such scandals respecting the proceedings of Illinois' courts to appear in its columns. I will here give entire only one of the many articles sent to the Boston papers in reply. This article was headed,

THE REPLY OF THE REPORTER OF MRS. PACKARD'S TRIAL, TO REV. THEOPHILUS PACKARD'S CHARGE OF MISREPRESENTATION.

"*To the Editors of the Boston Daily Advertiser:*—

In the supplement of the Boston Daily Advertiser of May 3d, appears a collection of certificates, introduced by Rev. Theophilus Packard; which requires a notice from me. These certificates are introduced for one or two purposes. First, either to prove that the report of the trial of Mrs. Elizabeth Packard, held before the Hon. C. R. Starr, Judge of the Second Judicial Circuit of the State of Illinois, on the question of her insanity, as published in the "Great Drama," is false; or, secondly, to prove to the readers of the Advertiser that Mr. Packard is not so bad a man as those who read the trial would be likely to suppose him to be.

In determining the truth of the statements of any number of persons relative to any given subject, it is always profitable to inquire who the persons that make the statements are, what is their relation to the subject-matter, and what their means of information.

I entered upon the defence of Mrs. Packard without any expectation of fee or reward, except such as arises from a consciousness of having discharged my duty toward a helpless and penniless woman, who was either indeed insane, or was most foully dealt with by him who had sworn to love, cherish and protect her. I was searching for the truth. I did then no more and no less than I should do for any person who claimed that their sacred rights were daily violated, and life made a burden most intolerable to be borne, by repeated wrongs.

The report was made from written notes of the testimony taken during the trial. And this is the first time I ever heard the correctness of the report called in question. It would be very unlikely that I should make an incorrect report of an important case, which I knew would be read by my friends and business acquaintances, and which (if incorrect) would work a personal injury. Policy and selfish motives would prevent me from making an incorrect report, if I was guided by nothing higher.

The first certificate presented is signed by Deacon A. H. Dole, and Sibyl T. Dole, who are the sister and brother-in-law of Mr. Packard, and, as the trial shows, his *co-conspirators;* J. B. Smith, another of his deacons, who was a willing tool in the transaction; and Miss Sarah Rumsey, another member of his Church, who went to live with Mr. Packard when Mrs. Packard was first kidnapped. Let Jeff. Davis be put on trial, and then take the certificates of Mrs. Surratt, Payne, Azteroth, Arnold, Dr. Mudd and George N. Saunders, and I am led to believe they would make out Jeff. to be a "Christian President," whom the barbarous North were trying to murder. Their further certificate "that the disorderly demonstrations by the furious populace, filling the Court House while we were present at the said trial, were well calculated to prevent a fair trial," is simply bosh, but is on a par with the whole certificate. It is a reflection upon the purity of our judicial system, and upon our Circuit Court, that they would not make at home. And I can only account for its being made on the supposition that it would not be read in Illinois. "The furious populace" consisted of about two hundred ladies of our city who visited the trial until it was completed, because they felt a sympathy for one of their own sex, whose treatment had become notorious in our city. The conspirators allege that Mrs. Packard is insane. They each swore to this on the trial, but a jury of twelve men after hearing the whole case, upon their oaths said in effect they did not believe these witnesses, for by their verdict they found her SANE.

The second certificate is from Samuel Packard. It is a sufficient answer to this to say that he is the son of Mr. Packard, and entirely under his father's control, and that it is apparent upon the document that the boy never wrote a word of it.

Then follows a certificate from Lizzie, who takes umbrage because I called her in the report the "little daughter" of Mrs. Packard, and is made to say pertly she was then *fourteen.* She then acted like a good daughter, who loved her mother dearly, and her size and age never entered into the consideration of the audience of ladies whose hearts were touched and feelings stirred, till the fountain of their tears was broken, by the kind and natural emotions which were then exhibited by the mother and daughter. When Mrs. Packard was put in the hospital Lizzie was about ten years old, and a thinking public will determine what judgment she could then form about her mother's "religious notions" and her "insanity," "to the great sorrow of all our family."

One word further upon the certificate of Thomas P. Bonfield, and I will close. He says that the trial commenced very soon after the writ of habeas corpus was served on Mr. Packard, and therefore he could not obtain his evidence, and was prevented from obtaining the attendance of Dr. McFarland, Superintendent of the Insane Hospital of Illinois. Dr. McFarland was the only witness whose attendance Mr. Packard's counsel expressed a desire for that was not present. They had his certificate that Mrs. Packard was insane, which they used as evidence, and which went to the jury. The defence had no opportunity for cross-examination, while Mr. Packard thus got the benefit of McFarland's evidence that she was insane, with no possibility of a contradiction. What more could he have had if the witness had been present?

The certificate further states that "a large portion of the community were more intent on giving Presbyterianism a blow than on investigating, or leaving the law to investigate, the question of Mrs. Packard's insanity." Well, what did the "feelings" of the community have to do with the court and jury? You selected the jury. You said they were good men. If not good, you could have rejected them. The presiding judge is a member of the Congregational Church, which is nearly allied to the Presbyterian. Five of the twelve jurymen were regular attendants of the Presbyterian Church. No complaint was then made that you could not have a fair trial. If Packard believed he could not, the statute of Illinois provides for a change of venue, which petition for a change of venue you had Mr. Packard sign, but which you concluded not to present, because you thought it would *not* be granted. If you thought it would not be granted, it was because you did not have a case that the venue could be changed, because when the proper affidavit is made for a change of venue, the Court has no power to refuse the application. The trial was conducted as all trials are conducted in Boston or in Illinois, and the verdict of the jury pronounced Mrs. Packard sane.

The published report of the trial is made. It no doubt presents Mr. Packard and his confederates in a very unfavorable light, but it is just as they presented themselves. If they do not like the picture they should not have presented the original.

STEPHEN R. MOORE.

KANKAKEE, ILL., MAY 16, 1865.

CONCLUSION.

In view of the above facts and principles on which this argument of "Self-defence from the charge of Insanity" is based, I feel sure that the array of sophisms which Mr. Packard may attempt to marshall against it, will only be like arguing the sun out of the heavens at noon-day. He is the only one who has ever dared to bring personal evidence of insanity against me, so far as my knowledge extends. Others believe me to be insane, but it is on the ground of his *testimony*, not from personal proof, by my own words and actions, independent of the coloring *he* has put upon them.

For example, I find he has reported as proof of my insanity, "that I have punished the children for obeying him." Had this been the case, in the sense in which he meant it to be understood, it would look like an insane, or at least very improper, act. But it is not true that I ever punished a child for obeying their father; but on the contrary, have exacted implicit obedience to their father's wishes and commands, and have even enforced this, my own command, by punishments, to *compel* them to respect their father's authority, by obeying his commands.

But this I have also done. I have maintained the theory, by logic and practice both, that a mother had a right to enforce her own reasonable commands—that her authority to do so was delegated to her by God himself, and not by her husband—and that this right to command being delegated to her by God himself, as the God given right identified with her maternity, the husband had no right to interfere or usurp this God bestowed right from the wife. But on the contrary, it was the husband's duty, as the wife's God appointed protector, to see that this right was defended to the wife by his authority over the children, requiring of them obedience to her commands, as one whose authority they must respect. Yes, I have trained my children to respect my authority as a God delegated authority, equal in power, *in my sphere*, to their father's God delegated authority. And farther, I have taught them, that I had no right to go out of *my sphere* and interfere with their father's authority in his sphere; neither had their father a right to trespass upon my sphere, and counter order my commands. I maintain, that the one who commands is the only rightful one to countermand. Therefore, the father has no right to countermand the mother's orders, except *through her;* neither has the mother a right to countermand the father's order, except through *him*. Here is the principle of "equal rights," which our government is bound to respect. And it is because they do not respect it, that my husband has usurped all my maternal rights, thus proving himself traitor, not only to his own manliness, but traitor to the principles of God's government.

But as this is a volume of facts, rather than theories, I will add one fact in vindication of my assertion, that I uniformly taught my children to respect their father's authority. When I was incarcerated in my prison, my oldest son, Theophilus, was in the post-office in Mt. Pleasant, Iowa, as clerk, and had not seen me for two years. His regard for me was excessive. He had been uniformly filial, and very kind to me, and therefore when he learned that his loving mother was a prisoner in a lunatic asylum, he felt an unconquerable desire to see me, and judge for himself, whether I was really insane, or whether I was the victim of his father's despotism. His father, aware of this feeling, and fearing he might ascertain the truth respecting me, by some means, sent him a letter, commanding him not to write to his mother now in the asylum, and by no means visit her there, adding, if he did so, he should disinherit him.

Theophilus was now eighteen years of age, and, as yet, had never known what it was to disobey either his father's or mother's express commands. But now his love for his mother led him to question the justice of this seemingly arbitrary command, and he, fearful of trusting to his own judgment in this matter, sought advice from those who had once been Mr. Packard's church members and deacons in Mt. Pleasant, and from all he got the same opinion strongly defended, that he had a right to disobey *such* a command. He therefore ventured to visit his mother in her lonely prison home in defiance of his father's edict. I was called from my ward to meet my darling firstborn son in the reception room, when I had been in my prison about two months. After embracing me and kissing me with all the fondness of a most loving child, and while shedding our mutual tears of ectasy at being allowed once more to meet on earth, he remarked, "Mother, I don't know as I have done right in coming to see you as I have, for father has forbid my coming, and you have always taught me never to disobey my father."

"Disobeyed your father!" said I. "Yes, I have always taught you it was a sin to disobey him, and I do fear you have done wrong, if you have come to see me in defiance of your father's command.

You know we can never claim God's blessing in doing wrong, and I fear our interview will not be a blessing to either of us, if it has been secured at the price of disobedience to your father's command."

Here his tears began to flow anew, while he exclaimed, "I was afraid it would prove so! I was afraid you would not approve of my coming! But, mother, I could not bear to feel that you had become insane, and I could not believe it, and would not, until I had seen you myself; and now I see it is just as I expected, you are not insane, but are the same kind mother as ever. But I am sorry if I have done wrong by coming."

I wept. He wept. I could not bear to blame my darling boy. And must I? was the great question to be settled. "My son," said I, "let us ask God to settle this question for us," and down we both kneeled by the sofa, and with my arm around my darling boy, I asked God if I should blame him for coming to see me in defiance of his father's order. While asking for heavenly wisdom to guide us in the right way, the thought came to me, "go and ask Dr. McFarland."

I accordingly went to the Doctor's parlor, where I found him alone, reading his paper. I said to him, "Doctor, I have a question of conscience to settle, and I have sought your help in settling it, namely, "has my son done wrong to visit me, when his father has forbid his coming, and has threatened to disinherit him if he did? He has the letter with him showing this to be the case."

After thinking a moment, the Doctor simply replied, "Your son had a *right* to visit his mother!"

O, the joy I felt at this announcement! It seemed as if a mountain had been lifted from me, so relieved was I of my burden. With a light heart I sought my sobbing boy, and encircling my arms about his neck, exclaimed, "Cheer up! my dear child, you had a *right* to visit your mother! so says the Doctor."

Why was this struggle with our consciences? Was it not that we had trained them to respect paternal authority? Can testimony, however abundant, change this truth into a falsehood?

That principle of self-defence, which depends wholly on certificates and testimonials, instead of the principle of right, truth and justice, is not able to survive the shock which the revelation of truth brings against it. A lie, however strongly fortified by testimonials and certificates, can never be transformed into a truth. Neither can the truth, however single, and isolated, and alone, be its condition, can never be transformed into a lie, nor crushed out of existence. No.

The truth will stand alone, and unsupported. Its own weight, simply, gives it firmness to resist all shocks brought against it, to produce its overthrow. Like the house built upon a rock, it needs no props, no certificates, to sustain it. Storms of the bitterest persecution may beat piteously upon it, but they cannot overthrow it, for its foundation is the rock of eternal truth. But lies, are like the house built upon the sand. While it does stand, it needs props or certificates on all sides, to sustain it. And it cannot resist the storm even of a ventilating breeze upon it, for it must and will fall, with all its accumulated props, before one searching investigation; and the more props it has so much the more devastation is caused by its overthrow.

And here I wish to add, that it was not because Mr. Packard was a minister, that bigotry had power thus to triumph over his manliness, but because he was a man, liable to be led astray from the paths of rectitude as other human beings are. The ministerial office does not insure men against the commission of sins of the darkest hue, for the ministry is composed of men, who are subject to like frailties and passions as other men are; and ministers, like all other men, must stand just where their own actions will place them, not where their position ought always to find them. They ought to be men whose characters should be unimpeached. But they are not all so. Neither are all other men what they should be in their position. It is as much the duty of the minister to be true to himself—true to the instincts of his God-like nature, as it is other men. And any deviation from the path of rectitude which would not be tolerated in any other man, ought not to be tolerated in a minister. In short, ministers must stand on a common level with the rest of the human race in judgment. That is, they, like others, must stand just where their own conduct and actions place them. If their conduct entitles them to respect, we should respect them. But if their conduct makes them unworthy of our respect and confidence, it is a sin to bestow it upon them; for this very respect which we give them ander such circumstances, only countenances their sins, and encourages them in iniquity, and thus puts their own souls in jeopardy, as well as reflects guilt on those who thus helped them work out their own destruction, when they ought to have helped them work out their own repentance for evil doing.

AN APPEAL TO THE GOVERNMENT.

As my case now stands delineated by the foregoing narrative, all the States on this continent can see just where the common law places all married women. And no one can help saying, that any law that can be used in support of such a persecution, is a disgrace to any government—Christian or heathen. It is not only a disgrace, a blot on such a government, but it is a crime, against God and humanity, to let confiding, trusting woman, be so unprotected in law, from such outrageous abuses.

Mr. Packard has never impeached my *conduct* in a single instance, that I know of; neither has he ever charged me guilty of one insane *act*—except that of teaching my children doctrines which I believed, and he did not! This is all he ever alleges against me. He himself confirms the testimony of all my friends, that I always did discharge my household duties in a very orderly, systematic, kind, and faithful manner. In short, they maintain that I, during all my married life, have been a very self-sacrificing wife and mother, as well as an active and exemplary co-worker with him in his ministerial duties.

Now I have mentioned these facts, not for self-glorification, but for this reason, that it may be seen that *good conduct*, even the best and most praiseworthy, does not protect a married woman from the most flagrant wrongs, and wrongs, too, for which she has no redress in the present laws. If a man had suffered a tithe of the wrongs which I have suffered, the laws stand ready to give him redress, and thus shield him from a repetition of them. But not so with me. I must suffer not only this tithe, with no chance of redress, but ten times this amount, and no redress then. I even now stand exposed to a life-long imprisonment, so long as my husband lives, while I not only have never committed any crime, but on the contrary, have ever lived a life of self-sacrificing benevolence, ever toiling for the best interests of humanity.

Think again. After this life of faithful service for others, I am thrown adrift, at fifty years of age, upon the cold world, with no place on earth I can call home, and not a penny to supply my wants with, except what my own exertion secures to me. Why is this? Because he who should have been my protector, has been my robber, and has stolen all my life-long earnings. And yet the law does not call this stealing, because the husband is legally authorized to steal from the wife without leave or license from her! Now, I say it is a poor rule that don't work both ways. Why can't the wife steal all the husband has. I am sure she can't support herself as well as he can, and the right of justice seems to be on our side, in our view.

But this is not what we want; we don't wish to rob our husbands, we only want they should be stopped from robbing us. We just ask for the reasonable right to use our own property as if it were our own, that is, just as we please, just according to the dictates of our own judgment. And when we insist upon this right, we dont want our husbands to have power to imprison us for so doing, as my husband did me. It was in this manner that I insisted upon my right to my property, with this fatal issue resulting from it.

While the discussions in our Bible-class were at the culminating point of interest, Mr. Packard came to my room one day and made me the following proposition: "Wife," said he, "how would you like to go to your brother's in Batavia, and make a visit?"

Said I, "I should like it very well, since my influenza has in some degree prostrated my strength, so that I need a season of rest; and besides, I should like an excuse for retiring from this Bible-class excitement, since the burden of these discussions lies so heavily upon me, and if it is not running from my post of duty, I should like to throw off this mental burden also, and rest for a season at least."

He replied, "You have not only a perfect right to go, but I think it is your duty to go and get recruited."

"Very well," said I, "then I will go, and go, too, with the greatest pleasure. But how long do you think I had better make my visit?"

"Three months."

"Three months!" said I, "Can you get along without me three months? and what will the children do for their summer clothes without me to make them?"

"I will see to that matter; you must stay three months, or not go at all."

"Well, I am sure I can stand it to rest that length of time, if you can stand it without my services. So I will go. But I must take my baby and daughter with me, as they have not fully recovered from their influenzas, and I should not dare to trust them away from me."

"Yes, you may take them."

"I will then prepare myself and them to go just as soon as you see fit to send us. Another thing, husband," said I, "I shall want ten dollars of my patrimony money to take with me for spending money." (This patrimony was a present of $600.00 my father had recently sent me for my especial benefit, and I had put it into Mr. Packard's hands for safe keeping, taking his note on interest as my only security, except with this note he gave me a written agreement, that I should have not only the interest, but any part of the principal, by simply asking him for it whenever I wanted it. When he absconded he took not only all this my money patrimony with him, but also stole all my notes and private papers likewise.)

"This you can't have," said he.

"Why not? I shall need as much as this, to be absent three months with two sick children. I may need to call a Doctor to them, and, besides, my brother is poor, and I am rich comparatively, and I might need some extra food, such as a beef-steak, or something of the kind, and I should not like to ask him for it. And besides, I have your written promise that I may have my own money whenever I want it, and I do want ten dollars of it now; and I think it is no unreasonable amount to take with me."

"I don't think it is best to let you have it. I shan't trust you with money."

"Shan't trust me with money! Why not? Have I ever abused this trust? Do not I always give you an exact account of every cent I spend? And I will this time do so; and besides, if you cannot trust it with me, I will put it into brother's hands as soon as I get there, and not spend a cent but by his permission."

"No, I shall not consent to that."

"One thing more I will suggest. You know Batavia people owe you twelve dollars for preaching one Sabbath, and you can't get your pay. Now, supposing brother 'dun' and get it, may I not use this money if I should chance to need it in an emergency; and if I should not need any, I won't use a cent of it? Or, I will write home to you and ask permission of *you* before spending a dollar of it."

"No. You shall neither have any money, nor have the control of any, for I can't trust you with any."

"Well, husband, if I can't be trusted with ten dollars of my own money under these circumstances, and with all these provisions attached to it, I should not think I was capable of being trusted with two sick children three months away from home wholly dependent on a poor brother's charities. Indeed, I had rather stay at home and not go at all, rather than go under such circumstances."

"You shall not go at all;" replied he, in a most excited, angry, tone of voice. "You shall go into an Insane Asylum!"

"Why, husband!" said I; "I did not suspect *such* an alternative. I had rather go to him penniless, and clotheless even, than go into an Asylum!"

"You have lost your last chance. You *shall* go into an Asylum!" And so it proved. It was my last chance. In a few days I was kidnapped and locked up in my Asylum prison for life, so far as *he* was concerned.

Now, I ask any developed man, who holds property which is rightfully his own, and no one's else, how he would like to exchange places with me, and be treated just as I was treated. Now, I say it is only fair that the law makers should be subject to their own laws. That is, they should not make laws for others, that they would not be willing to submit to themselves in exchange of circumstances. Just put the case to yourselves, and ask how would you like to be imprisoned without any sort of trial, or any chance at self-defence, and then be robbed of all your life earnings, by a law which women made for your good (?) as your God appointed protectors! O, my government—the men of these United States—do bear with me long enough to just make our case your own for one moment, and then let me kindly ask you this question.

Won't you please stop this robbery of our inalienable right to our own property, by some law, dictated by some of your noble, manly hearts? Do let us have a *right* to our own home—a *right* to our own earnings—a *right* to our own patrimony. A right, I mean, as *partners* in the family firm. We do not ask for a separate interest. We want an identification of interests, and then be allowed a legal right to this common fund as the *junior partners* of this company interest. We most cheerfully allow you the rights of a senior partner; but we do not want you to be senior, junior, and all, leaving us no rights at all, in a common interest.

Again, we true, natural women, want our own children too—we can't live without them. We had rather die than have them torn from us as your laws allow them to be. Only consider for one moment, what your laws are, in relation to our own flesh and blood. The husband has all the children of the married woman secured to himself, to do with them just as he pleases, regardless of her protests, or wishes, or entreaties to the contrary; while the children of the single women are all given to her as her right by nature! Here the maternal nature of the single woman is respected and protected, as it should be; while the nature of the married woman is ignored and set at naught, and the holiest instinct of woman is trampled in the dust of an utter despotism. In other words, the legitimate offspring of the wife are not protected to her, but given to the husband, while the illegitimate offspring of the unmarried women are protected to her. So that the only way to be sure of having our maternity respected, and our offspring legally protected to us, is to have our children in the single instead of the married state!

With shame I ask the question, does not our government here offer a premium on infidelity? And yet this is a Christian government! Why can't the inalienable rights of the lawful wife be *as much* respected as those of the open prostitute? I say, why? Is it because a woman has no individuality, after she is joined to a man? Is her conscience, and her reason, and her thoughts, all lost in him? So my case demonstrates the *law* to be, when practically tested.

And does not this legalized despotism put our souls in jeopardy, as well as our bodies, and our children? It verily does. It was to secure the interests of my immortal soul, that I have suffered all I have in testing these despotic laws. I would have succumbed long ago, and said I believed what I did not believe, had it not been that I cared more for the safety of my own soul, than I did the temporal welfare of my own dear offspring.

I could not be true to God, and also true to the mandates of a will in opposition to God. And whose will was to be my guide, my husband's will, or God's will? I deliberately chose to obey God rather than man, and in that choice I made shipwreck of all my earthly good things.

And one good thing I sorely disliked to lose, was my fair, untarnished reputation and influence. This has been submerged under the insane elements of this cruel persecution. But my character is not lost, thank God! nor is it tarnished by this persecution. For my character stands above the reach of slander to harm. Nothing can harm this treasure but my own actions, and these are all guided and controlled by Him, for whose cause I have suffered so much. Yes, to God's grace alone, I can say it, that from the first to the last of all my persecutions, I have had the comforting consciousness of duty performed, and an humble confidence in the approval of Heaven. Strong only in the justice of my cause, and in faith in God, I have stood *alone*, and defied the powers of darkness to cast me down to any destruction, which extended beyond this life. And this desperate treason against manliness which has sought to overwhelm me, may yet be the occasion of the speedier triumph of my spiritual freedom, and that also of my sisters in like bondage with myself.

The laws of our government most significantly requires us, "to work out our own salvation with much fear and trembling," lest the iron will which would hold us in subjection, should take from us all our earthly enjoyments, if we dare to be true to the God principle within us. So bitter has been my cup of spiritual suffering, while passing through this crucible of married servitude, that it seems like a miracle almost, that I have not been driven into insanity, or at least misanthropy by it. But a happy elasticity of temperament conspired with an inward consciousness of rectitude, and disinterestedness, has enabled me to despise these fiery darts of the adversary, as few women could.

And I cherish such a reverence for my nature, as God has made it, that I cannot be transformed into a "man-hater." I thank God, I was made, and still continue to be, a "man-lover." Indeed, my native respect for the manhood almost approaches to the feeling of reverence, when I consider that man is God's representative to me—that he is endowed with the very same attributes and feelings towards woman that God has—a protector of the weak, not a subjector of them. It is the exceptions, not the masses of the man race, who have perverted or depraved their God-like natures into the subjectors of the dependent. The characteristic mark of this depraved class is a "woman-hater," instead of a "woman-lover," as God, by nature made him. This depraved class of men find their counterpart in those women, who have perverted their natures from "men-lovers," into "men-haters." And man, with a man-hating wife, may need laws to protect his rights, as much as a woman, with a woman-hater for her husband. Laws should take cognizance of *improper actions*, regardless of sex or position.

All we ask of our government is, to let us stand just where our actions would place us, without giving us either the right or power to harm any one, not even our own husbands. At least, give us the power to defend ourselves, legally, against our husband's abuses, since you have licensed him with almost Almighty power to abuse us. And it will be taking from these women-haters no right to take from them the right to abuse us. It may, on the contrary, do them good, to be compelled to treat us with justice, just as you claim that it will do the slave-holder good, to compel him to treat his slave with justice. It is oppression and abuse alone we ask you to protect us against, and this we are confident you will do, as soon as you are convinced there is a need or necessity for so doing. And I will repeat, it is for this purpose that I have, in this pamphlet, delineated a subjected wife's true, legal position, by thus presenting my own personal, individual, experience for your consideration.

In summing up this argument, based on this dark chapter of a married woman's bitter experience of the evils growing out of the law of married servitude, I would close with a Petition to the Legislatures of all the States of this Union, that they would so revolutionize their statute laws, as to expunge them entirely from that most cruel and degrading kind of despotism, which identifies high, noble woman as its victim. Let the magnanimity of your holy, God-like natures, be reflected from your statute books, in the women protective laws which emanate from them. And may God grant that in each and all of these codes may soon be found such laws as guarantee to married woman a *right* to her own home, and a *right* to be the mistress of her own household, and a *right* to the guardianship of her own minor children.

In other words, let her be the legally acknowledged mistress of her own household, and a co-partner, at least, in the interests and destiny of her own offspring. Let the interests of the maternity be *as much* respected, at least, as those of the paternity; and thus surround the hallowed place of the wife's and mother's sphere of action, with a fortress so strong and invincible, that the single will of a perverted man cannot overthrow it. For home is woman's proper sphere or orbit, where, in my opinion, God designed she should be the sovereign and supreme; and also designed that man should see that this sphere of woman's sovereignty should be unmolested and shielded from any invasions, either foreign or internal. In other words, the husband is the God appointed agent to guard and protect woman in this her God appointed orbit. Just as the moon is sovereign and supreme in her minor orbit, being guarded and protected there by the sovereign power of the sun, revolving in his mighty orbit.

The appropriate sphere of woman being the home sphere, she should have a legal right here, secured to her by statute laws, so that in case the man who swore to protect his wife's rights here, perjures himself by an usurpation of her inalienable rights, she can have redress, and thus secure that protection in the *law*, which is denied her by her husband.

In short, woman needs legal protection *as a married woman*. She has a right to be a married woman, therefore she has a right to be protected *as a married woman*. If she cannot have protection as a married woman, it is not safe for her to marry; for my case demonstrates the fact, that the good conduct of the wife is no guarantee of protection to her; neither is the most promising developments of manhood, proof against depravity of nature, approximating very near to the point of "total depravity," and then woe to that wife and mother, who has no protection except that of a totally depraved man!

But, some may argue, that woman is already recognized in several of the States as an individual property owner, and as one who can do business on a capital of her own, independent of her husband. Yes, we do most gratefully acknowledge this as the day star of hope to us, that the tide is even now set in the right direction. But allow me to say, this does not reach the main point we are aiming to establish, which is, that woman should be a legal *partner* in the family firm, not a mere appendage to it. This principle of separating the interests of the married pair is not wholesome nor salutary in its results. It tends towards an isolation of interests; whereas it is an identification of interests, which the marriage contract should form and cement. We want an equality of rights, so far as copartners are concerned. These property rights should be so identified as to command the mutual respect of partners, whose interests are one and the same. In short, the wife should be the junior partner, and law should recognize her as such, by protecting to her the rights of a junior partner, and her husband should be the legally constituted senior partner of the family firm. Then, and only till then, is she his companion on an equality, in legal standing, with her husband, and sharing with him the protection of that government, which she has done so much to sustain; which government is based on the great fundamental principle of God's government, namely, an equality of rights to all accountable moral agents. Our government can never echo this heavenly principle, until it defends "equal rights," independent of sex or color.

APPENDIX.

REV. SAMUEL WARE'S CERTIFICATE TO THE PUBLIC.

"THIS is to certify that the certificates which have appeared in public in relation to my daughter's sanity, were given upon the conviction that Mr. Packard's representations respecting her condition were true, and were given wholly upon the authority of Mr. Packard's own statements. I do therefore certify that it is now my opinion that Mr. Packard has had no cause for treating my daughter Elizabeth as an insane person.

SAMUEL WARE.

Attest, OLIVE WARE,
AUSTIN WARE.

SOUTH DEERFIELD, AUG. 21, 1866."

The reader should be informed that the above certificate was given after I had been a member of my father's family for six months, thus affording him ample opportunity to judge of my real condition, by his own personal observation, since Mr. Packard, and his co-conspirator, Dr. McFarland, the Superintendent of the Asylum, both insist upon it, that I am now in just the same condition in reference to my sanity, that I was when I was kidnapped and forced into my prison. Therefore, when my own dear father's eyes were fully opened to see the deception that had been employed to secure his influence in support of this cruel conspiracy, he felt conscience bound to give the above certificate in vindication of the truth. Another evidence of my Father's entire confidence in my sanity is found in the fact that about this time he re-wrote his will, and so changed it that, instead of now giving me my patrimony "in trust" as before, he has bestowed it upon me, his only daughter, in precisely the same manner, and upon equal terms every way with my two only brothers.

MRS. PACKARD'S ADDRESS TO THE ILLINOIS LEGISLATURE.

GENTLEMEN OF ILLINOIS GENERAL ASSEMBLY:

Thankful for the privilege granted me, I will simply state that I desire to explain my bill rather than defend it, since I am satisfied it needs no defense to secure its passage by this gallant body of gentlemen.

I desire to make this public statement of some of the facts of my personal experience, relative to my incarceration in Jacksonville Insane Asylum, that you, the law-makers of this State, may see from the standpoint of my own individual wrongs, the legal liabilities to which all married women and infants have been exposed for the last sixteen years, to false imprisonments in Jacksonville Insane Asylum, under the act passed in 1851, viz. :

"Married women and infants who, in the judgment of the Medical Superintendent," (meaning the Superintendent of Illinois State Hospital for the Insane,) "are evidently insane or distracted, may be entered or detained in the hospital, on the request of the husband of the woman or the guardian of the infant, *without* the evidence of insanity required in other cases."

This act was nominally repealed in 1865 ; but, practically, is still existing, in retaining those who have been previously entered without evidence of insanity, and in receiving others, regardless of the law of '65, which demands a fair trial of all before commitment. In short, the present law is not in all cases enforced, but this unjust law is still in practical force in many instances.

Therefore, your petitioners, men of the first legal character and standing in Chicago, in asking for the repeal of this unjust law, not only ask for the enforcement of the new law by a penalty, but also that a jury trial may be forthwith extended to the unfortunate victims of this unjust law, who are now confined in Jacksonville Insane Asylum.

In detailing the practical working of this law in my case, I must rely upon your good sense to pardon the egotistical character of the following statement.

I am a native of Massachusetts, the only daughter of an orthodox clergyman of the Congregational denomination, and the wife of a Congregational clergyman, who was preaching to a Presbyterian Church in Manteno, Kankakee Co., Ill., when this legal persecution commenced.

I have been educated a Calvinist, after the strictest sect, but as my reasoning faculties have been developed by a thorough, scientific education, I have been led, by the simple exercise of my own reason and common sense, to endorse theological views, in conflict with my educated belief and the creed of the church with which I am connected. In short, from my present standpoint, I cannot but believe that the doctrine of total depravity, (which is the great backbone of the Calvinistic system,) conflicts with the dictates of reason, common sense, and the Bible.

And, gentlemen, the only crime I have committed is to dare to be true to these, my honest convictions, and to give utterance to these views in a Bible class in Manteno, at the special request of the teacher of that class, and with the full and free consent of my husband.

But the popular endorsement of these new views by the class and the community generally, led my husband and his Calvinistic Church to fear, lest their Church creed would suffer serious detriment by this license of private judgment and free inquiry, and as these liberal views emanated from his own family, and he, (for reasons best known to himself,) declining to meet me on the open arena of argument and free discussion, chose, rather, to use this marital power which your laws license him to use, and as this unjust law permits, and got me imprisoned at Jacksonville Insane Asylum, without evidence of insanity, and without any trial, hoping, as he told me, that by this means he could destroy my moral influence, and thereby defend the cause of Christ, as he felt bound to do!

It was under these circumstances I was legally kidnapped, as your laws allow, and imprisoned three years at Jacksonville, simply for claiming a right to my own thoughts. The first intimation I had of this legal exposure, was by two men entering my room, on the 18th of June, 1860, and kidnapping me. Two of his Church-members, attended by Sheriff Burgess of Kankakee, took me up in their arms and carried me to the wagon, and thence to the cars, in spite of my lady-like protests, and regardless of all my entreaties for some sort of trial before imprisonment.

My husband replied, "I am doing as the laws of Illinois allow me to do—you have no protection in law but myself, and I am protecting you now; it is for your good I am doing this; I want to save your soul; you don't believe in total depravity; I want to make you right."

"Husband," said I, "have not I a right to my opinion?"

"Yes, you have a right to your opinions if you think right."

"But does not the constitution defend the right of religious tolerance to all American citizens?"

"Yes, to all citizens it does defend this right, but you are not a citizen; while a married woman, you are a legal nonentity, without even a soul in law. In short, you are dead as to any legal existence, while a married woman, and therefore have no legal protection as a married woman."

Thus I learned my first lesson in that chapter of "common law," which denies to married women a legal right to their own individuality or identity.

Here I was taken from my little family of six children, while my babe was only eighteen months old, while in the faithful discharge of all my duties as wife and mother, having done all my own work for twenty-one years, besides educating our own children, and nearly fitting our oldest son for college; in perfect health and sound mind, and forced into an imprisonment of an indefinite length, without the mere form of a trial, and without any chance at self-defense.

True, my husband did even more than this "unjust law" demands, for he did get the certificates of two orthodox physicians that I was insane—like Henry Ward Beecher, and Horace Greeley, and Spurgeon, and three-fourths of the religious community; and, besides, he obtained the names of forty others, mostly his own Church members, who thus co-conspired to sustain their minister in this mode of defending the cause of Christ against the contagious influence of dangerous heresies and fatal errors.

The influence of the community outside of the Church was thrown into the opposite scale entirely; but their influence was overpowered by the majesty of the law, added to the dignity of the pulpit. I was conveyed by Sheriff Burgess, Deacon Dole and Mr. Packard to your State Hospital, in defiance of the indignant community who had assembled at the depot in large crowds to defend me. Dr. Simmington, the Methodist minister at Manteno, remarked to me, "Mrs. Packard, you will not be there long," and plainly intimated that, in his opinion, no man was fit for his position who would retain such an inmate as myself.

Dr. McFarland, of course, was obliged to receive me on this superabundant testimony that I was an insane person, although he apologized to me afterwards for receiving me at all, and for four months he treated me himself, and caused me to be treated, with all the respect of a hotel boarder. He even trusted me with the entire charge of a carriage load of insane patients, and the care of my own team, fourteen times; sometimes I would be absent nearly a half day on some pleasant excursion to the fair-grounds or cemetery, and he never expressed the least solicitude for our safe return. Indeed, he trusted me almost in every situation he would trust the matron.

But, at the expiration of this time, with no change whatever in my deportment, I forfeited all his good-will and favors, by presenting him a written reproof for his abuse of his patients, which was afterwards printed, wherein I told him I should expose him when I got out, unless he treated his patients with more justice.

He then removed me from the best ward to the worst, where were confined the most dangerous class of patients, and instructed his attendants to treat me just as they did the maniacs, and be sure to keep me a close prisoner, and on no account to allow me to leave the ward, and compel me to sleep in a dormitory with from three to six crazy patients, where my life was exposed, both night as well as day, with no room of my own to flee to for safety from their insane flights and dangerous attacks.

I have been dragged around this ward by the hair of my head by the maniacs; I have received blows from them that almost killed me. My seat at the table was by the side of Mrs. Triplet, the most dangerous and violent patient in the whole ward, who almost invariably threatened to kill me every time I went to the table. I have had to dodge the knives and forks and tumblers and chairs which have been hurled in promiscuous profusion about my head, to avoid some fatal blow. I have begged and besought Dr. McFarland to remove me to some place of safety, where my life would not be so exposed, only to see him turn, speechless, away from me! I have endured the scent and filth of a ward, from which my delicate, sensitive nature revolts in loathsome disgust, until I had had time to clean the whole ward with my own hands, before it could be a decent place for human beings to inhabit.

From this eighth ward I was not removed until I was discharged, two years and eight months from the day I was consigned to it. I did not set my foot upon the ground in the mean time, although, for the last part of my imprisonment there, Dr. McFarland exchanged some of the noisiest and most boisterous patients for a more quiet class.

I have been threatened with the screen-room, and this threat has been accompanied with the flourish of a butcher knife over my head, for simply passing a piece of johnny-cake through a crack under my door to a hungry patient, who was locked in her room to suffer starvation as her discipline for her insanity.

I have heard a fond and tender mother begging and pleading, for one whole night and part of a day, for one drink of cold water, but all in vain! simply because she had annoyed her attendant, by crying to see her darling babe and dear little ones at home. I finally persuaded the matron, Mrs. Waldo, to interpose, and give her a drink of water.

There was but one of all the employees at that Asylum whom the Dr. could influence to treat me, personally, like an insane person. This was Mrs. De La Hay. Besides threatening me with the screen-room, as I have stated, she threatened to jacket me for speaking at the table.

One day, after she had been treating her patients with great injustice and cruelty, I addressed Mrs. McKonkey, who sat next to me at the table, and in an undertone remarked, "I am thankful there is a recording angel present, noting what is going on in these wards;" when Mrs. De La Hay, overhearing my remark, exclaimed in a very angry tone, "Mrs. Packard, stop your voice! if you speak another word at the table I shall put a straight jacket on you!"

Mrs. Lovel, one of the patients, replied, "Mrs. De La Hay, did you ever have a straight jacket on yourself?"

"No, my position protects me! but I would as soon put one on Mrs. Packard as any other patient, 'recording angel' or no 'recording angel,' and Dr. McFarland will protect me in doing so, too!"

The indignant feeling of the house soon became so demonstrative, in view of the treatment I was receiving, that the Dr. seemed compelled to discharge Mrs. De La Hay to defend his own character from the charge of abusing me, and Mrs. De La Hay soon after became insane, and a tenant of Jacksonville poor-house.

He cut me off from all written communication with the outside world, except under the strictest censorship, and made it a dischargeable offence of his employees to permit me to have any means of communication with the outside world. He has refused Mrs. Judge Thomas and other friends, whom he knew desired to comfort me with human sympathy and some choi viands, admission into my presence, and has put them off with the inquiry, "why do you wish to single out Mrs. Packard from the other patients, to administer to her comfort?" and when asked by his guests, who often mistook me for the matron, "why he kept so intelligent a lady in an Insane Asylum?" he would reply, "you must not take any notice of what a patient says!" And the reply he would make to my indignant friends at the hospital, who ventured sometimes to inquire " why are you treating Mrs. Packard in this manner?" has invariably been, " it is all for her good!."

Time will not allow me to detail my sufferings and persecutions at that hospital; I will only add, may the Lord forgive Dr. McFarland for the injustice I have suffered at his hands! And God grant that the legislature of 1867 may have the moral courage to effectually remove the liabilities to a repetition of wrongs like my own!

Various attempts were made by my Manteno friends to rescue me, but all in vain. My legal non-existence rendered it difficult to extend legal aid to a nonentity, except it come through the identity of my only legal protector, and so long as it was possible to cut me off from any direct application for deliverance, he could ward off the habeas corpus investigation they wished to institute, and as long as the Doctor claimed I was insane, so long this unjust law consigned me to legal imprisonment. My relatives and other friends applied to lawyers, judges and the Governor in my behalf, but all in vain, as these officers were only authorized to administer existing laws; they could neither repeal them nor act contrary to them. On the 18th of June, 1863, I was finally removed from my asylum prison, by order of the Trustees, as the result of a personal interview which Dr. McFarland kindly consented to grant me, and put again into the custody of my husband, who consigned me to a prison in my own house, claiming, as his excuse, that I was just as insane as when I was entered just three years previously, for I had neither recanted nor yielded my right to my identity: therefore, in the judgment of your superintendent, I am hopelessly insane, and am doomed, by his certificates, to a life-long imprisonment in the Insane Asylum at Northampton, Mass., and my husband was just on the point of starting with me for a consignment in that living tomb, when he was arrested by a writ of habeas corpus, issued by judge Starr, of Kankakee City, and used by my Manteno friends in defence of my personal liberty. I was now where I could make direct application, by passing a letter clandestinely through a crack in my window.

The trial lasted five days, and resulted in a complete vindication of my sanity, although his witnesses swore that it was evidence of insanity for a person to wish to leave a Presbyterian church and join a Methodist! A full account of this trial is found in this "Three Years Imprisonment for Religious Belief." It was reported by one of my lawyers, and is an impartial record of the whole case.

During the trial, Mr. Packard "fled his country" in the night, to avoid the danger of a mob retribution. He took with him all our personal property, even my own wardrobe and children, and rented our home, so that I found myself, at the close of court, homeless, penniless and childless.

And this, gentlemen, is legal usurpation, also, on the slavish principle of common law—the legal nonentity of the wife, the man and wife being one, and the one, the man! Gentlemen, we married women need emancipation; and will you not be the pioneer State in our Union, in woman's emancipation? and thus use my martyrdom for the identity of a married woman, to herald this most glorious of all reforms—married woman's legal emancipation, from that of a slave in law, to that of a partner and companion of her husband, in law, as she now is in society?

And, lest there be a misunderstanding on this subject, permit me here to explain what kind of slavery I refer to. This slavish position which the principles of common law assigns the married woman, is a relic of barbarism, which the progress of civilization will, doubtless, ere long, annihilate. In the dark ages, married woman was a slave to her husband, both socially and legally, but, as civilization has progressed, she has outgrown her social position—that of a slave—and is now regarded in society as the companion and partner of her husband. But the law has not progressed with civilization, so that married woman is still a slave, legally, while she is his companion, socially.

Man, we know, is woman's natural protector, and, in most instances, is all the protection a married woman needs. Still, as the laws are made for the exceptional cases, where man is not a law unto himself, what can be the harm in emancipating woman from this slavish position, so that she can receive governmental protection of her right to "life, liberty and the pursuit of happiness," as well as the marital protection? So, in case where the marital fails, she can have legal protection, while married as well as when single. Then when your darling daughter is called to exchange the paternal protection for the marital, she will not be obliged to alienate her right to governmental protection by this exchange of her natural protectors, but she, the tenderest and the best, can then claim of her government, while a married woman, the same protection of her rights as a woman, which your sons now claim as men.

The need of this radical change in married woman's legal position, is more fully elucidated in this book, which contains a detailed account of my persecutions in Illinois, when your State hospital was used, in my case, as an inquisition. My object in bringing these facts to your notice is to secure legislative action, where these facts show the need of action.

In conclusion, gentlemen of this Assembly, may I be allowed to read a few extracts from Dr. McFarland's published letters on this subject, showing, from his own words, his ground of self-defense.

The Doctor says: "All Mrs. Packard's wrongs, persecutions and sufferings, of every description, are utterly the creation of a diseased imagination."

Now, I ask, is this so? Can facts be transmuted into fiction by the simple assertion of one man? And is it a mere creation of a diseased imagination that has torn me from my helpless babe and deprived my darling children of a fond mother's tender care? Is it the mere creation of a diseased imagination to find that good conduct, not even the best, is any guarantee of protection to a wife and mother under Illinois laws?

Neither Dr. McFarland nor Mr. Packard himself, has ever denied one of the facts in the statement I have made; but as their only justification, they claim that I am insane—and the only proof of insanity they have ever brought in support of this opinion is, "her views of things," as the Doctor expresses himself, or, my private, individual opinions.

Now I wish to ask the gentlemen of this Assembly, if, for my using my right of opinion, or my right of private judgment, the public sentiment of this age is going to justify Illinois in keeping me a prisoner three years, under the subterfuge of insanity, based wholly upon my "views of things?"

Just consider, for one moment, the principle. Here my personal liberty, for life, hangs suspended wholly on the opinion of this one man, whom policy or interest might tempt to say I was insane when I was not; for this law expressly states that the class I represent may be imprisoned without evidence of insanity, and without trial!

Just make the case your own, gentlemen: would it be easy for you to realize that it was a mere creation of your imagination to have two men take you by force from your business and family, without evidence of insanity and without trial, and your kidnappers claim as their only justification, that you are insane on some point in your religious belief, simply because Dr. McFarland says you are, and then lock you up for life, on his single testimony, without proof?

Now we, married women and infants, have had our personal liberty, for sixteen years, suspended on this one man's opinion; and possibly he may be found to be a fallible man, and capable of corruption, if we may be allowed to judge of this great man from the standpoint of his own words and actions.

Now, if the Doctor was required to prove his patients insane, from their own conduct, there would be a shadow of justice attached to his individual judgment; but while this law allows him to call them insane, and treat them as insane, without evidence of insanity, where is the justice of such a decision?

You do not hang a person without proof from the accused's own actions that he is guilty of the charge which forfeits his life. So the personal liberty of married women should not be sacrificed without proof that they are insane, from their own conduct.

When Dr. McFarland has brought forward one proof from my own conduct, by one insane act of my own, in support of his position, I will then say he has cause for calling me an insane person; but until that time arrives, I claim he is begging the question entirely, in calling me an insane person, without one evidence to sustain his charge.

Gentlemen, it is not merely for my own self-defence from this unpleasant charge, that I lay this argument before you, but it is that you may see, from my standpoint, how exceedingly frail is the thread on which our reputation for sanity is suspended, and how very liable married women and infants are to be thus falsely imprisoned in Jacksonville Insane Asylum.

If my testimony might be allowed to add weight to this suspicion or presumption, I would state that, to my certain knowledge, there were married women there when I left, more than three years since, who were not insane then at all, and they are still retained there, as hopelessly insane patients, on the simple strength of the above ground of evidence; and it is my womanly sympathy for this class of prisoners that has moved me to come, alone, from Massachusetts, in the depth of winter, to see if I could not possibly induce this legislature to compassionate their case: for it is under your laws, gentlemen, I have suffered, and they are still suffering, and it is to this legislature of 1867 that we apply for a legal remedy; and we confidently trust you will vindicate the honor of your State in the action you take upon this subject. We trust you will not only have the manliness and moral courage to repeal this unjust law, forthwith, but also extend, promptly, a just trial to its wronged and injured victims.

Again, Dr. McFarland writes: "Mr. Packard is suffering from a cause which only gather his church and the public about him, in the bonds of a generous sympathy."

I reply to this assertion by stating a few simple facts. Mr. Packard's church and people in Manteno, Illinois, withdrew from him their confidence and support, while I was incarcerated, instead of gathering about him, because public sentiment would not tolerate him, as a minister, with this stigma upon him; and it was the fear of lynch law which drove him from this State during the court, to seek shelter and employment in Massachusetts, his native State. There he succeeded in securing a place as stated supply, by ignoring the decision of your court, and by misrepresenting the west to be in such a semi-barbarous state that it was impossible to get a just decision at any legal tribunal in this uncivilized region, where, he tells them, "a large portion of community were more intent on giving Presbyterianism a blow, than in investigating the question of Mrs. Packard's insanity!"

He occupied his new field in Sunderland, Mass., fifteen months, when I returned to my father's house in Sunderland, on a visit, and the result was, my personal presence, together with the facts in the case, upset him, so that neither Sunderland nor any other society in New England can be induced to employ him in defiance of enlightened public sentiment. Indeed, the public sentiment of New England has so blighted and withered his ministerial influence, that the remark of a lawyer in Worcester, Mass., made a few months since, reflects his true social position there, at present. Said he, "there is not a man in New England, neither do I think there is one man in the United States, who would dare to stand the open defender of Mr. Packard in the course he has taken, and in view of the facts as they are now known to exist."

Now I would like to ask Dr. McFarland, where are to be found these "bonds of generous sympathy" to which he refers? in the region of the west, or in the east?

Here, where the Doctor's assertion is found to be plainly contradicted by facts, can his simple assertions be relied upon as infallible testimony and infallible authority?

Again, another extract, and I am done.

Dr. McFarland writes, "I have no question but that Mrs. Packard's committal here was as justifiable as in the majority of those now here."

Now if this statement of your superintendent is true, viz.: that I am a fair specimen of the majority of his patients, then the Doctor himself must admit that the majority of inmates there are capable of assuming a self-reliant position, and, instead of being supported there as State paupers, as I was during my imprisonment of three years, ought they not to be liberated, and supporting themselves and their families as I am now doing?

Mr. Packard has become an object of charity since he cast me penniless upon the world, while I have, without charity, not only supported myself, but have already become voluntarily responsible for his support, and the support and education of my children, from the avails of my own hard labor, since my discharge from my prison; while at the same time, he will not allow me to live in the house with my dear children, lest my heresies contaminate them!

Now, Gentlemen, is it not better that I be thus employed, selling my books for their support, rather than be held as your State's prisoner and State's pauper simply because my "views of things" do not happen to coincide with your Superintendent's views of things?

It is true, and, gentlemen, your Superintendent's own statement verifies it, that I am not the only one who has been so unjustly imprisoned there, and in the name and behalf of those now there, I beg of this body that you extend to such a fair trial or a discharge. Really, the claims of humanity and the honor of your State both demand that my case stimulate the Illinois legislature of 1867 to provide legal safeguards against false commitments like my own.

Permit me here to add, that although I have come from Massachusetts to Illinois at my own expense, without money and without price, for the express purpose of bringing these claims of oppressed humanity to your notice, I do not demand nor ask for any remuneration for my false imprisonment in your State institution, nor for any personal redress of those legal wrongs which have deprived me of my reputation, my home, my property, my children, my liberty; but I do ask that the legal liabilities to such like outrages may be effectually removed by this legislature, and that the justice of a trial by jury may be forthwith extended to those now in that asylum, who have been consigned to an indefinite term of imprisonment, without any trial.

Gentlemen of this assembly, in view of the facts now before you, please allow me the additional privilege of adding a few suggestions.

You see it has become a demonstrated fact that I, a minister's wife, of Illinois, have been three years imprisoned in your State, by your laws, simply because I could not tell a lie—that is, I could not be false to my own honest convictions; and since I simply claim the right to be an individual instead of a parasite, or an echo of others' views, I am branded by your laws as hopelessly insane!

Is it not time for you to legislate on this subject, by enacting laws which shall make it a crime to treat an Illinois citizen as an insane person simply for the utterance of opinions, no matter how absurd those opinions may be to others? Opinions cannot harm the truth, nor the individual, especially if they are absurd or insane opinions.

But for irregularities of conduct, such as my persecutors have been guilty of, the law ought to be made to investigate. Imprisonment for religious belief! What is it but treason against the vital principle of this American Government, viz.: religious toleration?

Would that I could have claimed protection under the banner of my country's flag, while a citizen of Illinois. But no; this unjust statute law has consigned me to the reign of despotism. And so are all my married sisters in Illinois liable to this consignment, so long as this barbarous law is in force.

And O! the horrors of such a consignment! Only think of putting your own delicate, sensitive daughter through the scenes I have been put through. Do you think she would have come out unharmed? God only knows. But this I do know: that it is one principle of ethics, that a person is very apt to become what they are taken to be. You may take the sanest person in the world, and tell them they are insane, and treat them as your Superintendent treats them there—it is the most trying ordeal a person can pass through and not really become insane.

And most reverently does Mrs. Packard attribute it to God's grace alone, for carrying her safely through this most awful ordeal, unharmed, and—I am almost tempted to add—God himself could not have done this thing without the strictest conformity on my part, to His own laws of nature, in connection with a well-balanced organization. As it is, to God's grace alone. I say it, I am a monument for the age—a standing miracle, almost, of the power of faith to shield one from insanity, by having come out unharmed, through a series of trials, such as would crush into a level with the beasts, I may say, any one, who did not freely use this antidote.

Here let me make one practical suggestion. Is that kind of treatment which causes insanity the best adapted to cure insanity?

O. my brothers! my gallant brothers! will you not protect us from such liabilities? Will you not have the manliness to grant to us, married women, the legal right to stand just where our own actions will place us, regardless of our views of things, or our private opinions? that is, may we not have the privilege of being legally protected, as you are, in our rights of opinion and conscience, so long as our good conduct deserves such protection?

We have an individuality of our own, which is sacred to ourselves; will you not protect our personal liberty, while in the lawful, ladylike exercise of it? for personal liberty is a boon of inestimable value to ourselves as well as you, and by guarding our liberty against false commitment there, you may have fortified the personal liberty of some of Illinois' best and sanest class of citizens, whose interests are now vitally imperiled by this unjust law.

Yes, gentlemen, I, their representative, now stand legally exposed to be kidnapped again, and hid for life in some lunatic Asylum; and since no laws defend me, this may yet be done. Should public sentiment—the only law of self-defence I have—endorse the statements of this terrible conspiracy against the personal liberty and stainless character of an innocent woman, I may yet again be entombed, to die a martyr for the Christian principle of the identity of a married woman. Three long years of false imprisonment does not satisfy this lust for power to oppress the helpless. No; nothing but a life-long entombment can satisfy the selfhood of my only legal protector.

O! I do want laws to protect me, and, as an American citizen, I not only ask, but I demand that my personal liberty shall depend upon the decision of a jury—not upon the verdict of public sentiment, or forged certificates, either.

My gallant brothers, be true to my cause, if false to me. Be true to woman! defend her as your weak, confiding sister, and Heaven shall reward you; for God is on her side, "and he always wins who sides with God."

Fear not; fear nothing so much as the sin of simply not doing your duty. Maintain your death grapple in defence of the heavenborn principles of liberty and justice to all human kind, especially to woman. Emancipate her! for above this cross hangs suspended a crown, of which even our martyred Lincoln's crown of negro emancipation is but a mere type and shadow in brilliancy. And God grant that this immortal crown of unfading honor may be the rightful heritage—the well-earned reward of Illinois' gallant sons, as embodied in their legislators.

And all we have to ask for Dr. McFarland is, that you not only allow, but require this great man to stand just where his own actions will place him, regardless of his position, or the opinion of his enemies or his friends.

Gentlemen, permit me also to say, that when you have once liberated the sane inmates of that hospital, and effectually fortified the rights of the sane citizens of Illinois against false commitments there, you will have taken the first progressive step in the right direction, in relation to this great humanitarian reform. And here I will say, that from what I do know of the practical workings of the internal machinery of that institution, as seen from behind the curtain, from the standpoint of a patient, and from what I know of the personal and private character of Illinois Statesmen, I predict it will not be the last.

And, notwithstanding the temporary disfigurement of Illinois' proud escutcheon by this foul stain of religious persecution, which, I regret to say, it now has upon it, may God grant that the present statesmen of Illinois may yet so fully vindicate its honor, as that the van of this great humanitarian reform may yet be heralded to the world in the action of Illinois representatives, as embodied in this legislature of 1867.

I hold myself in readiness, gentlemen, to answer any questions, or perform any service in behalf of this cause you may desire of me; and, as an incentive to your acting efficiently in this matter, I will state that several legislatures in New England are watching eagerly the result of my application to you, this winter, and they have engaged me to report to them the result.

I desire, therefore, an opportunity to vindicate your character bebefore these legislatures, on the basis of your own actions, for, after you know of the existence of this barbarous law, and its direct application to me, one of its wronged and injured victims, as you now do, I shall no longer be able to plead your ignorance of the existence of such a law, as your vindication from the charge of barbarism, and you must know that the intelligence of the whole civilized world cannot but call a State barbarous in its legislation, so long as this black and cruel law has an existence, even in continuing to hold its victims in its despotic grasp.

I know, gentlemen, that since 1865, I can plead that you have nominally repealed it, but so long as this law of '65 is without a penalty to enforce it, it is only a half law, or in other words, it is merely legislative advice—it is not a statute law, and so long as you do retain its injured victims in their false imprisonment, you have not repealed it.

Now, gentlemen, much as I would like to gratify the wishes of a member of your House, in erasing the record of this law from my book, on the ground of its having been already repealed, I cannot conscientiously do it so long as that institution continues to receive inmates without any trial by jury, or retains those who have never had any such trial.

No, gentlemen; this law and its application to me, cannot be obliterated, for it has already become a page of Illinois' history, which must stand to all coming time, as a living witness against the legislation of Illinois in the nineteenth century. There is one way, and only one, by which you can redeem your State from this foul blot of religious persecution which now desecrates your nationality in the estimation of the whole civilized world, and that is by such practical repentance as this bill demands. This done, I can then, and only till then, vindicate the character of Illinois statesmen, on the ground of their own honorable acts.

In an appendix to this book, you will then find not only Mrs. Packard's appeal to Illinois' legislature of 1867, but also the noble manly response of its legislators, as echoed by their own honorable acts. But, should you, for any reason, choose to turn a deaf ear to this appeal in defense of your injured citizens, I shall not rest until I have made this same appeal to the people of this State, and asked from them the justice I am denied from their representatives. And should I be denied there, I shall go to work single-handed and alone, in liberating this oppressed class, by the habeas corpus act, before I shall feel that my skirts are washed from the guilt of hiding these public sins against humanity, which I know to have existence in the State of Illinois.

And can you blame me for this manifestation of my heart sympathy for my imprisoned sisters? Can a sensitive woman feel a less degree of sympathy for her own sex, when she knows, as I do from my own bitter experience, the injustice they are daily and hourly now receiving in that dismal prison?

And O! if you or your darling daughter were in their places, would you feel like reproaching me as a fanatic, for thus volunteering in your defence? No; you would not. But I should reproach myself, and so must a just God reproach me, should I dare to do less; for there is a vow recorded in the archives of high Heaven, that Mrs. Packard will do all in her power to do, for the deliverance of these victims of injustice, if God will but grant her deliverance. I am delivered! my vow stands recorded there! Shall this vow be a witness against me, or shall it not?

Gentlemen of this Assembly, I shall try to redeem that pledge, and so far as you are concerned, my work is now done. Yours remains to be done. God grant you may dare to do right! that you may have the moral courage to dare to settle this great question, just upon its own intrinsic merits, independent of the sanity or the insanity of its defender.

Very respectfully submitted to the General Assembly of Illinois, now in Session, by—

Mrs. E. P. W. PACKARD.

SPRINGFIELD, ILLINOIS, February 12th, 1867.

The result of this appeal was the passage of the "Personal Liberty Bill," entitled "An Act for the Protection of Personal Liberty."

ACTION OF ILLINOIS LEGISLATURE ON THIS SUBJECT.

AN ACT in relation to Insane persons and the Illinois State Hospital for the Insane.

SECTION 1. *Be it enacted by the People of the State of Illinois, represented in the General Assembly:* That the circuit judges of this Satte are hereby vested with power to act under and execute the provisions of the act passed on the 12th of February, 1853, entitled "An act to amend an act entitled 'an act to establish the Illinois State Hospital for the Insane,'" in force March 1st, 1847, in so far as those provisions confer power upon judges of county courts; and no trial shall be had of the question of sanity or insanity before any judge or court, without the presence or in the absence of the person alleged to be insane. And jurors shall be freeholders and heads of families.

SEC. 2. Whenever application is made to a circuit or county judge, under the provisions of this act and the act to which this is an amendment, for proceedings to inquire into and ascertain the insanity or sanity of any person alleged to be insane, the judge shall order the clerk of the court of which he is judge to issue a writ, requiring the person alleged to be insane to be brought before him, at the time and place appointed for the hearing of the matter, which writ may be directed to the sheriff or any constable of the county, or the person having the custody or charge of the person alleged to be insane, and shall be executed and returned, and the person alleged to be insane brought before the said judge before any jury is sworn to inquire into the truth of the matters alleged in the petition on which said writ was issued.

SEC. 3. Persons with reference to whom proceedings may be instituted for the purpose of deciding the question of sanity or insanity, shall have the right to process for witnesses, and to have witnesses examined before the jury; they shall also have the right to employ counsel or any friend to appear in their behalf, so that a fair trial may be had in the premises; and no resident of the State shall hereafter be admitted into the hospital for the insane, except upon the order of a court or judge, or of the production of a warrant issued according to the provisions of the act to which this is an amendment.

Sec. 4. The accounts of said institution shall be so kept and reported to the general assembly, as to show the kind, quantity and cost of any articles purchased for use; and upon quarterly settlements with the auditor, a list of the accounts paid shall be filed, and also the original vouchers, as now required.

Sec. 5. All former laws conflicting with the provisions of this act are hereby repealed, and this act shall take effect on its passage.

Approved February 16, 1865.

Two years practice under this law developed its inability to remove the evils it was designed to remedy. This law, having no penalty to enforce it, was found to be violated in many instances, as it was ascertained to be a fact that Dr. McFarland was constantly receiving patients under the old law of 1851, which this law had nominally repealed. Therefore, a petition was sent to the legislature of 1867, signed by I. N. Arnold, J. Young Scammon, and thirty-six other men of the first legal standing in Chicago, asking for the practical repeal of the old law of 1851, by the enforcement of the new law of 1865.

The old law of 1851 is as follows, viz.: "Married women and infants who, in the judgment of the medical superintendent, (meaning the Superintendent of the Illinois State Hospital for the Insane,) are evidently insane or distracted, may be entered or detained in the hospital on the request of the husband of the woman, or the guardian of the infant, *without* the evidence of insanity required in other cases."

The legislature was led to see that by the practical enforcement of this unjust law, the personal liberty of married women and infants was still imperiled, and also that the law of 1865 did not relieve the wronged and injured victims of this unjust law, now imprisoned at Jacksonville Insane Asylum. Therefore, the legislature of 1867 passed the following "Act for the protection of Personal Liberty."

AN ACT for the Protection of Personal Liberty.

Section 1. *Be it enacted by the People of the State of Illinois, represented in the General Assembly:* That no superintendent, medical director, agent or other person, having the management, supervision or control of the Insane Hospital at Jacksonville, or of any hospital or asylum for insane and distracted persons in this State, shall receive, detain or keep in custody at such asylum or hospital any person who has not been declared insane or distracted by a verdict of a jury and the order of a court, as provided by an act of the general assembly of this State, approved February 16, 1865.

SEC. 2. Any person having charge of, or the management or control of any hospital for the insane, or of any asylum for the insane in this State, who shall receive, keep or detain any person in such asylum or hospital, against the wishes of such person, without the record or proper certificate of the trial required by the said act of 1865, shall be deemed guilty of a high misdemeanor, and liable to indictment, and on conviction be fined not more than one thousand dollars, nor less than five hundred dollars, or imprisoned not exceeding one year, nor less than three months, or both, in the discretion of the court before which such conviction is had: *provided*, that one half of such fine shall be paid to the informant, and the balance shall go to the benefit of the hospital or asylum in which said person was detained.

SEC. 3. Any person now confined in any insane hospital or asylum, and all persons now confined in the hospital for the insane at Jacksonville, who have not been tried and found insane or distracted by the verdict of a jury, as provided in and contemplated by said act of the general assembly of 1865, shall be permitted to have such trial. All such persons shall be informed by the trustees of said hospital or asylum, in their discretion, of the provisions of this act and of the said act of 1865, and on their request, such persons shall be entitled to such trial within a reasonable time thereafter: *provided*, that such trial may be had in the county where such person is confined or detained, unless such person, his or her friends, shall, within thirty days after any such person may demand a trial under the provisions of said act of 1865, provide for the transportation of such person to, and demand trial in the county where such insane person resided previous to said detention, in which case such trial shall take place in said last mentioned county.

SEC. 4. All persons confined as aforesaid, if not found insane or distracted by a trial and the verdict of a jury as above, and in the said act of 1865 provided, within two months after the passage of this act, shall be set at liberty and discharged.

SEC. 5. It shall be the duty of the State's attorneys for the several counties to prosecute any suit arising under the provisions of this act.

Sec. 6. This act shall be deemed a public act, and take effect and be in force from and after its passage.

Approved March 5th, 1867.

The public will see that, under the humane provisions of this act, all the inmates of every insane asylum in the State of Illinois, whether public or private, who have been incarcerated without the verdict of a jury that they are insane, are now entitled to a jury trial, and unless this trial is granted them within sixty days from the 5th of March, 1867, they are discharged, and can never be incarcerated again without the verdict of a jury that they are insane. No person can be detained there after sixty days, who has not been declared insane by a jury.

It is thus that the barbarities of the law of 1851 are wiped out by this act of legislative justice. Now, all married women and infants who have been imprisoned " without evidence of insanity," as this unjust law allows, and who are still living victims of this cruel law, will now be liberated from their false imprisonment, unless they have become insane by the inhumanity of their confinement. And if it is found by the testimony that they were sane when they were imprisoned, and that they have become insane by being kept there, is it humane to perpetuate the cause of their insanity, under the pretext that their cure demands it? Or, in other words, is that kind of treatment which caused their insanity the best adapted to cure their insanity?

This great question, who shall be retained as fit subjects for the insane asylum, is now to depend, in all cases, upon the decision of a jury; and each case must be legally investigated, as the law of 1865 directs.

ANOTHER ACT OF LEGISLATIVE JUSTICE—APPOINTMENT OF AN INVESTIGATING COMMITTEE.

Resolved, the Senate concurring, That a joint committee of three from this House and two from the Senate be appointed to visit the hospital for the insane, after the adjournment of the legislature, at such times as they may deem necessary, with power to send for persons and papers, and to examine witnesses on oath; that said committee be instructed thoroughly to examine and inquire into the financial and sanitary management of said institution; to ascertain whether any of the inmates are improperly detained in the hospital, or unjustly placed there, and whether the inmates are humanely and kindly treated, and to confer with the trustees of said hospital in regard to the speedy correction of any abuses found to exist, and to report to the Governor, from time to time, at their discretion.

And be it further resolved, That said committee be instructed to examine the financial and general management of the other State institutions.

Adopted by the House of Representatives,

F. CORWIN, *Speaker.*

Concurred in by the Senate,·

WM. BROSS, *Speaker.*

The following gentlemen compose the committee: Hon. E. Baldwin, Farm Ridge, LaSalle county; Hon. T. B. Wakeman, Howard, McHenry county; Hon. John B. Ricks, Taylorville, Christian county, on the part of the House of Representatives. Hon. Allen C. Fuller, Belvidere, Boone county; Hon. A. J. Hunter, Paris, Edgar county, on the part of the Senate.

www.ingramcontent.com/pod-product-compliance
Lightning Source LLC
Chambersburg PA
CBHW030309170426
43202CB00009B/939